The Meaning of Life

ALSO BY MARC MAUER

Race to Incarcerate

Race to Incarcerate:
A Graphic Retelling (with Sabrina Jones)

Invisible Punishment:
The Collateral Consequences of Mass Imprisonment
(edited with Meda Chesney-Lind)

ALSO BY ASHLEY NELLIS

A Return to Justice: Rethinking Our
Approach to Juveniles in the System

The Meaning of Life

THE CASE FOR ABOLISHING
LIFE SENTENCES

Marc Mauer and Ashley Nellis

Featuring six portraits of lifers
by Kerry Myers

NEW YORK
LONDON

Requests for permission to reproduce selections from this book
should be mailed to: Permissions Department, The New Press,
120 Wall Street, 31st floor, New York, NY 10005.

Parts of chapter 7, "The Racial Meaning of Life," reproduced with
permission from Marc Mauer and Ashley Nellis, "The Impact of Life
Imprisonment on Criminal Justice Reform in the United States," Dirk van
Zyl Smit and Catherine Appleton, eds., 2016, *Life Imprisonment and Human
Rights*, Hart Publishing, an imprint of Bloomsbury Publishing Plc.

Photograph of Willis X. Harris on page 169 by Alan Pogue.

Published in the United States by The New Press, New York, 2018
Distributed by Two Rivers Distribution

ISBN 978-1-62097-409-4 (hc)
ISBN 978-1-62097-410-0 (ebook)
CIP data is available

The New Press publishes books that promote and enrich public discussion and
understanding of the issues vital to our democracy and to a more equitable world.
These books are made possible by the enthusiasm of our readers; the support
of a committed group of donors, large and small; the collaboration of our many
partners in the independent media and the not-for-profit sector; booksellers, who
often hand-sell New Press books; librarians; and above all by our authors.

www.thenewpress.com

Composition by dix!
This book was set in Fairfield LH

Printed in the United States of America

2   4   6   8   10   9   7   5   3   1

In memory of Barbara Cartwright and Ahmad Rahman,
my mentors and friends
—MM

To Ruthie and Twyla, who light up my world
—AN

It is said that no one truly knows a nation until one has been inside its jails. A nation should not be judged by how it treats its highest citizens, but its lowest ones.

—Nelson Mandela

Contents

CONTENTS

The Meaning of Life

Introduction
Lessons of "The Birdman"

In the early part of the last century, Robert Stroud was considered one of the most notorious and dangerous individuals in the U.S. prison system. Born in Seattle, Stroud ran away from his abusive father at the age of thirteen. He settled in Alaska and became a pimp by the age of eighteen. In 1911, he was convicted of the brutal murder of a bartender who had allegedly not paid for the services of one of his prostitutes, and was sentenced to twelve years in prison.[1]

In federal prison, Stroud on various occasions stabbed other prisoners and attacked a hospital orderly. After being transferred to Leavenworth Federal Penitentiary, he got into an altercation in 1916 with a guard over a violation that would have prohibited a prison visit from his brother. In retaliation he fatally stabbed the guard in the prison cafeteria in front of 1,100 prisoners. He was convicted of the murder and sentenced to death by hanging, but in 1920 he received a commutation of sentence to life without parole from President Woodrow Wilson.

The name of Robert Stroud is not familiar to very many Americans today, but many more know of his fame as the *Birdman of Alcatraz*, played by Oscar-nominated Burt Lancaster in the 1962 film. Shortly after receiving his sentence commutation, Stroud came across an injured sparrow in the Leavenworth prison yard and took it back to his cell for care. Over time he collected three hundred canaries and, with the support of prison officials, studied their behavior in the adjoining prison cells that became his laboratory. His observations over many years led him to author two well-regarded books on canaries and to develop expertise on their diseases and treatment. Crime reporter Carl Sifakis regarded Stroud as "possibly the best-known example of self-improvement and rehabilitation in the U.S. prison."

Robert Stroud's personal transformation over time was remarkable and a testament to the ability of the human spirit to thrive under adverse circumstances. But it also raises fundamental questions about sentencing, redemption, and predicting human behavior, particularly in regard to those who have committed great harm to others.

On the day of his sentencing for murder in 1911 neither the judge nor anyone else in the courtroom would have thought that Robert Stroud would someday gain a national reputation as a contributor to scientific inquiry. Nor would anyone have thought that possible at the sentencing for his second murder, or at any time during his first decade of imprisonment.

And yet Robert Stroud clearly possessed the human capacity for transformation, in his case triggered by the simple act of caring for a wounded bird. Other people experience such transformations through the aid of a gifted teacher, the caring of a loved one, or a book that opens one's mind to new experiences and insights.

Sentences of life imprisonment are imposed for various reasons related to public safety and upholding societal values. To the extent that these goals are based on assumptions of future behavior, we should reflect on the difficulty of making such predictions. This does not suggest that every person convicted of a serious crime will turn out to be a Robert Stroud, but neither does it suggest that no one will overcome their transgressions.

American society is now at a moment of growing concern about the challenge of mass incarceration, a development described by many as "the civil rights issue of the twenty-first century." Critical voices span the political spectrum, and increasingly we hear calls for a substantial reduction in the prison population over the next decade. Many states and the federal government have enacted reforms designed to produce better outcomes for people returning home from prison or to avoid sentencing people to prison in the first place. But while a handful of states have achieved substantial reductions in their prison populations, the overall pace of decline is still quite modest, particularly when viewed against the nearly four-decade buildup of the prison system.

Many factors explain both the massive expansion of the prison system and the relatively modest pace of decarceration today. One of the most significant is the severity of punishment imposed on people sentenced to prison. Along with the death penalty, the broad use of life imprisonment is perhaps the most distinctive aspect of the American punishment system in relation to other industrialized nations. One of every seven people in prison in the United States—a total of more than two hundred thousand people—is currently serving a life prison term, more than the entire prison population in 1972, before the advent of mass incarceration.[2] This includes those serving life without the possibility of parole, those with the possibility of parole, and "virtual" lifers, as defined by a sentence of fifty years or more.

The implications of these figures for ending mass incarceration are quite stark. While much attention has appropriately been directed to the counterproductive War on Drugs of the past several decades, the portion of those incarcerated for a drug offense is only about 20 percent. (It is a higher percentage of the federal prison population, but only 20 percent of *all* incarcerated people). This is hardly trivial, and is troubling in many respects, but it makes clear that even if we were to legalize all drug-related behavior, this would not end mass incarceration.

Life imprisonment, along with the death penalty, also serves to exert upward pressure on sentencing for all offenses, not just serious crimes. Since sentencing structures are proportional, generally based on the severity of the crime, a higher upper bound created by sentences of life imprisonment inevitably leads to harsher punishments for auto theft, burglary, and other crimes.

While it is critical to examine the role of long-term sentences as a contributor to mass incarceration, it is equally important to assess the value of life sentences in promoting public safety. The best that can be said for long-term imprisonment is that it has had some effect on crime, but, as we will explore, the scale of that effect is far more modest than commonly believed. Further, due to the long-established finding that individuals "age out" of crime, the country is far past the point of diminishing returns for public safety, as lifers age in prison.

The widespread use of life imprisonment also fundamentally violates legal and human rights norms concerning the scale of punishment. Scholars across nations have called for a scale of punishment that is *no more than necessary* to accomplish the goals of sentencing. The use of life imprisonment in the United States goes well beyond that standard.

Finally, the massive use of life imprisonment poses a fundamental challenge to any notion of forgiveness and redemption. How do we decide as a community how much punishment is enough to promote public safety and to express societal condemnation of a person's illegal behavior? Americans generally frown at the thought of cutting off the hands of thieves, believing such barbaric behavior is not fitting for a modern society. Where, then, do we draw the line? At what point does punishment become barbaric? Is it at placing long-term prisoners in solitary confinement for months or years on end? Is it at housing life-sentenced prisoners hundreds of miles from home so as to make family visits virtually impossible? Is it providing little in the way of intellectual or cultural stimulation, or pathways to cope with the consequences of the crime that led to imprisonment? We may all draw the line at a different place along this continuum of punishment, but we nonetheless need to have a national dialogue about where that line should be drawn and why.

In our consideration of these issues, we must not forget about the people who have been harmed by the crimes underlying these sentences. Family members and friends of murder victims and those who have been assaulted or otherwise harmed are in need of comprehensive support to recover from their losses. The ways in which we do this as a society may include financial restitution, medical and psychological support, victim-offender mediation, and other services.

Ultimately, there should be no conflict between advocating for reduced prison terms for serious offenses and for greater support to those in our communities who have been victimized by crime. Achieving public safety is a process that involves multiple institutions within society and multiple approaches to changing behaviors. In the era of mass incarceration we have produced a distorted and counterproductive version of what that process should look like.

If the movement to end mass incarceration is to be successful, we will need to prioritize a challenge to the political culture and policies that have made the deep end of the American prison system a stain on the ideals of a democratic society. This fundamental human rights violation is not only counterproductive for public safety but lowers the moral standing of the United States in the eyes of the world. It is long past time to join the rest of the democratic world by scaling down the excessive nature of punishment that has become the hallmark of mass incarceration.

Life by the Numbers

At the start of the prison expansion era in the early 1970s, a total of two hundred thousand people were incarcerated in state and federal prisons. Today, more than that number are serving life sentences, with many effectively condemned to die in prison.

This figure, which accounts for one in seven of the total 1.5 million imprisoned population (not including those serving short sentences in jails), has become known only over the past decade. As campaigns to challenge mass incarceration have developed, much attention has focused on reversing the War on Drugs, the 1980s-era policies that produced a ten-fold increase in the number of people incarcerated for drug offenses. Important as those movements have been—and with some success in changing public policy—there has been virtually no public discussion of life imprisonment.

This gap was largely due to the lack of information on life sentences. The only data from that era were collected in a one-time survey of departments of corrections by the American Correctional Association in 1984. The total at the time of 34,000 people serving life sentences should have generated public discussion but remained largely unknown amid the ensuing "tough on crime" period.

A subsequent analysis in 1992 documented a doubling of the life-sentenced population to 69,000.[1] As with the 1984 analysis, this report also generated little public attention. In part this may have been due to the fact that both of these early reports provided only a total number of life sentences nationally and by state, with no demographic or offense breakdowns. Thus, there was no way of understanding the variation of life sentences by state, the range of offenses that could qualify for a life sentence, or the racial/ethnic impact of sentencing policies of the period.

Perhaps the most glaring omission of relevant data was the failure of the Bureau of Justice Statistics, the well-regarded research arm of the Department of Justice, to document the scale of life imprisonment. In part this reflected the large-scale lack of interest in studying the development of the policies we have since come to call mass imprisonment.

The Bureau of Justice Statistics has produced an annual prison count for state and federal prisons for more than four decades. Scholars today make good use of the substantial prison reports that assess trends in incarceration, provide detailed data on the offense breakdowns of individuals in prison, and track race and ethnicity data with increasing sophistication. But looking back at the 1980 report, for example, shows a four-page publication simply documenting the growth in the prison population from 1979 to 1980 and reporting the number of people held in local jails due to overcrowding in state prisons. With few exceptions, state-level reports were similarly perfunctory, given the scale of the incarceration growth at the time. Policymakers had no means of assessing the scale of prison admissions and releases, the amount of time prisoners were expected to serve, comparative recidivism rates, or many other policy-relevant factors. And if there was no information on sentencing patterns in general, there certainly was nothing about extreme sentencing such as life imprisonment.

Beginning in 2003 The Sentencing Project has undertaken a series of five national studies of the scope of life sentences, documenting truly shocking trends with broad significance for the scale of incarceration in the United States, for public safety concerns, and for the intersection of race and the criminal justice system.

Nearly five times the number of people are now serving life sentences in the United States as were in 1984, a rate of growth that has outpaced even the sharp expansion of the overall prison population during this period. Dramatic as this growth trend may be, international comparisons demonstrate just how unique the scale of life imprisonment is in the United States. A comprehensive 2016 international analysis of life imprisonment found that the number of people serving life imprisonment in the United States is higher than the *combined* total in the other 113 countries surveyed.[2] Researchers Dirk van Zyl Smit and Catherine Appleton estimate that the United States accounts for 40 percent of the world's total.[3]

The data also show people serve life sentences in the United States at a rate of 64 per 100,000 population, a figure greater than the incarceration rate for *all* categories of sentences in the Scandinavian nations of Denmark, Finland, and Sweden.

For much of this era, policy changes have driven the scale of life imprisonment up, even as serious crime has declined.

The Meaning of "Life"

Three types of life sentences can be imposed in an American courtroom: life *without* the possibility of parole (LWOP), life *with* the possibility of parole, and "virtual" life sentences, which we define as a prison term of at least fifty years. The federal government as well as every state except Alaska allows for some mix of life with or without parole sentencing, and all fifty states and the District of Columbia impose virtual life sentences.

Sentences of life without parole remove the possibility of release except in the increasingly rare event of gubernatorial clemency (or presidential clemency in the federal system). In forty-nine states, the District of Columbia, and the federal court system, life sentences are a sentencing option. In twenty-nine of these states and the federal government, life without the opportunity for parole is the only possible punishment for certain crimes,[4] typically first-degree homicide. One of every four people serving a life sentence—a total of more than fifty thousand people—is not eligible for parole. To place some perspective on this figure, fifty people were serving a sentence of life without parole in the United Kingdom as of 2015. Thus, the United States, which has about five times the population of the United Kingdom, has more than one thousand times the number of people serving life without parole.

More than half of the lifer population, 108,887 individuals, are serving life sentences *with* an opportunity for parole. In these cases, the state maintains the right to keep an individual in prison for the remainder of his or her life (e.g., a twenty-five-to-life sentence), but there is the potential for release after a specified period. Though a typical life with parole sentence results in release after a term of years, the politics and practices of parole have shifted in recent decades to narrow and delay prospects for release, resulting in a greater likelihood of life imprisonment until death.

The third category of life sentences consists of the 44,311 individuals serving "virtual" life sentences, defined as a sentence of at least fifty years. Included in these counts would be an individual who was sentenced to sixty years and is parole-eligible after thirty years, or someone sentenced to two separate terms of twenty-five years to be served consecutively. A prisoner with an indeterminate sentence that ranges from forty to fifty years would also be included in this count.

Who Is Serving Life Sentences?

While most of the people serving life sentences have been convicted of serious and/or violent crimes, a substantial number are serving life for nonviolent offenses. (And even those sentenced for a violent offense are often kept in prison long after they cease to

Table 1. State Totals: Life with Parole, Life Without Parole, and Virtual Life Sentences, 2016

State	Life with Parole	Life Without Parole	Virtual Life	Total	Prison Population	Percent of Prison Population
Alabama	3,895	1,559	650	6,104	25,037	24.4%
Alaska	0	0	400	400	4,701	8.5%
Arizona	1,181	504	624	2,309	42,685	5.4%
Arkansas	778	637	1,006	2,421	17,262	14.0%
California	34,607	5,090	994	40,691	129,805	31.3%
Colorado	2,131	667	785	3,583	20,246	17.7%
Connecticut	55	73	612	740	15,831	4.7%
Delaware	128	435	228	791	3,942	20.1%
Florida	4,086	8,919	1,161	14,166	99,938	14.2%
Georgia	7,533	1,243	601	9,377	53,169	17.6%
Hawaii	294	55	11	360	3,769	9.6%
Idaho	504	126	19	649	7,353	8.8%
Illinois	5	1,609	3,478	5,092	46,240	11.0%
Indiana	107	123	3,537	3,767	26,759	14.1%
Iowa	43	670	456	1,169	8,310	14.1%
Kansas	1,188	28	161	1,377	9,712	14.2%
Kentucky	804	111	594	1,509	22,425	6.7%

(continued on next page)

Table 1. State Totals: Life with Parole, Life Without Parole, and Virtual Life Sentences, 2016

State	Life with Parole	Life Without Parole	Virtual Life	Total	Prison Population	Percent of Prison Population
Louisiana	20	4,875	6,343	11,238	36,463	30.8%
Maine	0	64	72	136	2,243	6.1%
Maryland	2,803	338	1,017	4,158	21,442	19.4%
Massachusetts	959	1,018	61	2,038	8,795	23.2%
Michigan	1,317	3,804	590	5,711	42,406	13.5%
Minnesota	461	130	6	597	10,105	5.9%
Mississippi	595	1,470	348	2,413	18,751	12.9%
Missouri	1,767	1,144	525	3,436	32,399	10.6%
Montana	30	47	293	370	2,548	14.5%
Nebraska	96	265	408	769	5,364	14.3%
Nevada	2,329	569	339	3,237	13,662	23.7%
New Hampshire	157	83	26	266	2,867	9.3%
New Jersey	1,127	77	876	2,080	20,135	10.3%
New Mexico	442	1	608	1,051	7,194	14.6%
New York	9,260	275	354	9,889	52,344	18.9%
North Carolina	1,858	1,387	887	4,132	36,677	11.3%
North Dakota	40	30	10	80	1,795	4.5%

Table 1. State Totals: Life with Parole, Life Without Parole, and Virtual Life Sentences, 2016

State	Life with Parole	Life Without Parole	Virtual Life	Total	Prison Population	Percent of Prison Population
Ohio	5,955	560	170	6,685	50,443	13.3%
Oklahoma	2,021	887	682	3,590	28,946	12.4%
Oregon	434	118	185	737	14,601	5.0%
Pennsylvania	44	5,398	2,358	7,800	49,914	15.6%
Rhode Island	216	31	27	274	2,667	10.3%
South Carolina	1,094	1,117	329	2,540	21,597	11.8%
South Dakota	0	174	197	371	3,505	10.6%
Tennessee	1,910	336	1,317	3,563	20,115	17.7%
Texas	8,320	798	8,637	17,755	148,521	12.0%
Utah	1,940	64	—	2,004	6,405	31.3%
Vermont	107	14	—	121	1,508	8.0%
Virginia	1,239	1,338	—	2,577	38,701	6.7%
Washington	2,052	622	279	2,953	17,211	17.2%
West Virginia	362	286	100	748	7,019	10.7%
Wisconsin	970	225	218	1,413	22,557	6.3%
Wyoming	154	35	122	311	2,440	12.7%
Federal	1,249	3,861	1,610	6,720	191,476	3.5%
Total	**108,667**	**53,290**	**44,311**	**206,268**	**1,480,000**	**13.9%**

— = Data not available.

13

present any significant threat to public safety.) The racial and ethnic composition of the life-sentenced prison population mirrors the broad racial and ethnic disparities of the criminal justice system, only more so. And the scale of life imprisonment, including life without parole for juveniles, marks the United States as unique in the world.

Offense of Conviction

Individuals serving sentences of life imprisonment have generally been convicted of serious crimes. Fifty-nine percent of lifers are serving sentences for homicide, 17 percent for rape or sexual assault, 15 percent for aggravated assault, robbery, or kidnapping. While violent offenses account for the bulk of this population, 8 percent, or 17,120 people, have been convicted of a nonviolent offense. These include 5,300 people convicted of a drug offense and 4,700 people of a property offense.

In some states a significant portion of those sentenced have been convicted of nonviolent crimes. In South Carolina, for example, 9 percent of people serving life without parole have been convicted of either a drug or property offense, and in Alabama, this is the case for 7 percent. This is especially evident in the federal prison system, where more than two-thirds of the lifer population has been convicted of a nonviolent crime. Because of the high proportion of federal prisoners serving time for a drug offense (half the population, compared to one in six in state prisons) the number of lifers serving time for a drug offense is quite high as well. Of those serving life without parole, half are serving time for a drug offense.

Race and Ethnicity

As is the case of prison populations generally, the life-sentenced population is disproportionately comprised of people of color. Two-thirds of people serving life sentences are people of color, including nearly half (48 percent) who are African American, a total of one hundred thousand people. As a result, one of every five African Americans in prison is serving a life sentence.

The number of Latinos in the justice system has risen dramatically in recent years (though much of this increase is due to a rise in the general population), including among the life-sentenced population. Nearly one in six lifers (16 percent) are Latino, but the number ranges as high as 47 percent in New Mexico and 37 percent in California.

Juvenile Status

Nearly 12,000 life sentences have been imposed on individuals who were under the age of eighteen at the time of their offense, including about 2,300 sentenced to life without parole (though many of the latter are being resentenced due to Supreme Court decisions). Every state except Maine and West Virginia currently holds individuals serving a life sentence for crimes committed as juveniles. In seven states—Arkansas, Kansas, Kentucky, Maryland, Michigan, Missouri, and Pennsylvania—at least one in thirteen (8 percent) of the people serving a life sentence were under eighteen at the time of their offense. The United States is virtually alone among nations in sentencing juveniles to life imprisonment.

Trends over Time

For more than two decades in the United States, the overall rate of crime, and the rate of violent crime, has been declining substantially, and it is now about half of its level in 1993. Prison populations nationally have started to decline for the first time in four decades, with reductions as high as 30 percent in a handful of states.

Despite these trends, the number of people serving life

sentences has more than doubled, a 132 percent increase from 69,845 in 1992 to 161,957 in 2016. (These figures include sentences of life with and without parole, but not virtual life sentences, for which there is little historical data.) Within these overall increases, sentences of life without parole have grown most significantly, a 59 percent rise between 2003 and 2016, compared to an increase of 18 percent for sentences of life with parole in this period. There is also great variation in the scale of increase among the states when life with and without parole are examined separately. Colorado increased its parole-eligible life sentences from 943 to 2,131—a 126 percent rise—between 2003 and 2016. Life-with-parole sentences in Washington nearly quadrupled from 539 in 2003 to 2,052 in 2016. In all but two states life *without* parole figures have also increased between 2003 and 2016, from a low of a 10 percent increase in South Dakota to a high of a 433 percent increase in Ohio.

In some states the decline of parole-eligible life sentences masks the scale of the increase in life without parole. For example, Indiana lowered its life with parole population by 34 percent over this time from 161 individuals to 107, presumably through parole grants, but nearly doubled its life without parole population from 66 in 2003 to 123 in 2016. While this is clearly a trend toward harsher sentencing, the statistical result when viewed together is an overall life-sentence increase of only 1 percent. In other states, such as South Carolina, reductions in the overall prison population have come with a quickening of the pace of growth in life sentences: between 2003 and 2016 the state lowered its prison population by more than 11 percent but at the same time doubled its life without parole population. The growth in life without parole sentences is due in part to an increased reliance on these sentences for non-homicide crimes, constituting about one-third of the cases.

Women Lifers

The number of women serving life sentences has risen at a faster rate than for men in recent years. Between 2008 and 2016, women lifers increased by 20 percent, compared to a 15 percent increase for men. This trend parallels the disproportionate increase in women's incarceration overall since the 1980s, a function of the gendered impact on women of the War on Drugs and harsher sentencing policies.

There are no national figures on the number of life sentences being served by women whose physical, sexual, or psychological abuse precipitated the murder of the victim. One study of forty-two survivors of domestic abuse convicted of murder in California found that all but two were given life sentences: six were sentenced to life without parole, another fifteen received fifteen years to life. The remaining nineteen received life sentences with minimums that ranged from seven to ten years, but at the time of the study all these women had already served twenty-five years.[5]

A review of women in prison for homicide in Georgia found that more than half had been the victims of domestic abuse, and in nearly two-thirds of the cases in which a woman killed a partner, abuse was claimed to have occurred at the time of the crime.[6] These women often face the question from law enforcement and legal professionals, "Why didn't you just leave?" In addition to an insensitivity to the complexity that women face in trying to make a decision to leave, this assertion ignores the fact that the risk of additional injury or death at the hands of an abuser often increases after fleeing.[7]

Many battered women have received little help from the legal system, since many criminal justice professionals, including defense attorneys, have never understood or appreciated the significance of abuse. Sociologist Elizabeth Leonard writes that:

Many lawyers and investigators fail to adjust their approach to better fit the experiences of women. As a result, potentially exculpatory information is not investigated, crucial evidence remains unused, and women are left with no real defense. . . . Some accused women take the offered plea bargains to protect their children, to spare their families, to avoid the death penalty threatened by prosecutors, or to speed up what they see as the inevitable guilty verdict.[8]

Denise Dodson

Denise Dodson found her power in prison after the wreckage of an abusive relationship landed her there in her twenties to serve out a life sentence.

"Growing up I learned that if you are in a relationship like that you get out," she said during an interview from the prison where she resided for the past twenty-five years. Denise got out of that relationship, though, as often happens when proximity provides opportunity, her abusive ex-boyfriend turned stalker. "It didn't end there because he constantly sought me out. Everywhere I'd go I'd see him pop up and he'd always have an excuse as to why he was there."

But it was another traumatic event, a sexual assault when she was younger, that would become the catalyst for tragedy. In her late twenties, pregnant with her ex-boyfriend's child, she confided to her uncle one fateful day that she had been sexually assaulted several years earlier and identified her assailant. Doing so, she felt, unburdened her of a secret she had kept too long. The ex-boyfriend hadn't known about the assault, until Denise's uncle called and told him. The next day, the ex-boyfriend killed the man, and informed Denise about what he had done.

Charged with conspiracy to commit murder and as a principal to the crime, Denise maintains that she had no advance knowledge of the crime, nor did she encourage or conspire with her ex to kill the man. She believed that cooperating, telling the truth, including about the fact that she did not contact the authorities once she had learned what her ex-boyfriend had done, and explaining what happened, would set things right. She was wrong. Tried together with her ex, who apologized and tried to clear her, Denise was convicted and sentenced to life with the possibility of parole. "Long story short, I wound up here as a result of the choices he made as well as the choices I made because I could have very well reported it to authorities. I didn't. . . . My heart, I never wanted to be the reason people get in trouble, so I was busy safeguarding others as well as my own heart and I ended up here."

The severity of her sentence was shocking. "I walked around like, I can't believe this. Am I really in the midst of this?" Regrets about remaining silent at the time still made for some difficult nights, even twenty-five years later. "Yes, I have been angry. I have spent a lot of nights laying there thinking that I am a good person. I'm a good person, I didn't do anything that warranted a life sentence. To sit in here and think that you could possibly die inside these walls. . . . But I've overcome that, I've grown, I've learned, and I feel like it's time to go now."

The journey taught Denise many things about life and even more about herself. But maybe the most important lesson is that what happens to you in life matters less than how you respond to what happens. "So, I have often thought, God, what is it? What is it that you want me to see, that you want me to learn?" She believes she has found some answers, and in them found her power. One answer is education. "My mom was a school teacher and I remember sitting in an overcrowded classroom with few books, having to share old, stained texts with classmates." Denise once dreamed of going to college but knew the odds were not in her favor. "The expectations of success as a middle school student were just a dream.

But I still dreamed because I wanted to be a college student, but never felt equipped to do that."

Complicating matters, she dropped out of high school in her senior year because she was pregnant and ashamed. The dream of college was now painfully out of reach. Her path had suddenly taken a hard turn.

After sentencing and assignment to the Maryland Correctional Institute for Women, it took about six months for the reality to sink in. "I couldn't believe where I was and what was being said. It didn't connect," she recalled. Denise's first step was getting her high school diploma while simultaneously enrolling in therapeutic cognitive behavioral and transactional analysis courses. Calling the sessions "intensive," she explained that they took her back to her childhood to understand why she made the choices she made. "I feel more connected to things now. I understand a lot more. I am a fifty-three-year-old woman and, yeah, I get it."

Maryland Correctional Institute for Women provided an array of meaningful work and rehabilitation and education programs, and Denise soaked them up like a sponge. She began working in garment manufacturing, designing patterns and making clothes. Armed with her high school diploma and with her self-esteem growing, she sought and was assigned a job doing inventory control. It didn't take long for her skills and work ethic to be noticed, leading to a new assignment in data entry. After years of daily typing she developed carpal tunnel syndrome and was reassigned as a clerk. "I do different stuff because I've been there so long," she said, adding that her responsibilities are significant and varied.

A high school diploma and job training were not nearly enough, so Denise enrolled in and earned a certificate in a business management program—this, on her own time, after the workday was over. "I go to school after work," she said, a goal she worked toward for more than twelve years as she pursued a bachelor's degree. Denise also trained service dogs for fifteen years.

A normal day in prison began at 5 a.m.—showering, taking her service animal outside, going through a series of training commands before feeding, and getting ready for work. The dog was her constant companion, living with and going everywhere Denise went. There were seven training sessions during a day, and the training never stopped until it was complete, when the dog found a permanent home. She cried, while knowing the dog would improve someone's life, then welcomed a new puppy to begin the process again. The dog training, she readily admits, did as much for her as it did for the people for whom she trained them. "It has allowed me to open up and talk. Before, I couldn't do that, to speak up for myself. I was afraid of negative responses, so I just sat there and listened. Now I can speak for myself. It changed me. It has changed me as far as the outside world is concerned. I have so much respect for the animals and for people."

School was challenging. When the workday ended at 2:30, Denise did as she had for a dozen years and headed for class, which ended at 7 p.m. She took three classes a semester. If she had problems with a subject, she sought out tutors. The days were long, with Denise sometimes not returning to her cell until 8:30 in the evening. "You don't have enough time in a day. It really does take discipline."

In the evenings, Denise thought about her day as she climbed into bed. She is proud of herself because of her accomplishments, but more so because of whom she has become. "I think about my children and grandchildren. I let them know what I am learning, what is expected of them, and I have been able to teach them from here. It's sometimes hard to understand my purpose here, but I do know that I have grown. I share it with them so that they can be successful."

Her support system was extensive. Two of her sisters are Baltimore police officers, as are two of her nieces. Her mother is living, and her children are all successful. With no hesitation, she said that the hardest thing about being incarcerated for two and a half decades was leaving her children. She clearly remembers feeling the pain of the youngest holding on to her leg as the trial ended, asking when she would be back.

Then, Denise had no power. Things are different now. "I am ready for the world, ready for the job world. I am ready to play my part. I understand what is expected of me as a member of society. I understand my purpose and what I can do to help my family and my community. It took some time for me to understand. It's almost like prison sometimes creates a passion for purpose. I'm here. I'm in prison. I have a life sentence. My passion is to help other people—I don't care who you are—and to be the best person for my children. I am somebody, not a number. I will live, not just exist. That is who I am and who I will be."

In Maryland individuals serving life imprisonment can be released only through an executive action from the governor. In 2014, after an extensive interview with parole commissioners and a psychological assessment, Denise received a recommendation for release from the parole board. In February 2018 Governor Larry Hogan reduced her sentence to forty years, making her immediately parole-eligible. Shortly after, the Parole Board approved her release and Denise returned home to her family in March.

Policies That Drive Life Sentences

The large-scale use of life sentences is a relatively new phenomenon in the United States. Until 1970, only seven states had a provision for life without parole in their sentencing codes, whereas every state except Alaska now permits this punishment.

For most of the twentieth century, a life sentence in many states typically resulted in ten or fifteen years in prison. Louisiana, which has the nation's highest incarceration rate overall and holds more than 11,000 individuals serving life without parole, in years past released lifers after ten years on average. The federal system, which currently holds nearly seven thousand people on a life sentence, previously defined "life" as fifteen years, but since 1987 all life sentences have been imposed with no possibility of parole.

Policy choices, not criminal offending patterns, have produced the dramatic expansion in both the number of people serving life imprisonment and the years they must serve before being considered for release. While crime has gone through periods of both growth and decline in the past four decades, life sentences have continued to rise throughout this period.

A number of factors explain this unprecedented expansion. As the death penalty came under serious scrutiny in the 1970s some states adopted policies of life without parole so as to have a severe penalty available if the death penalty were struck down by the courts. The "tough on crime" era beginning in the 1980s led to harsher penalties across the board, including an expansion of the

Table 2. State Enactment of Life Without Parole Statutes

1970 and Earlier (7)	1972–1990 (26)	1991–2012 (17)
Massachusetts	Alabama	Arizona
Michigan	Arkansas	Florida
Mississippi	California	Georgia
Montana	Colorado	Indiana
Pennsylvania	Connecticut	Kansas
South Dakota	Delaware	Kentucky
West Virginia	District of Columbia	Minnesota
	Hawaii	Nebraska
	Idaho	New Jersey
	Illinois	New York
	Iowa	North Carolina
	Louisiana	North Dakota
	Maine	Ohio
	Maryland	Tennessee
	Missouri	Texas
	Nevada	Utah
	New Hampshire	Wyoming
	New Mexico	
	Oklahoma	
	Oregon	
	Rhode Island	
	South Carolina	
	Vermont	
	Virginia	
	Washington	
	Wisconsin	

scope of life sentences. This came about by enhancing the scale of habitual offender laws and adopting a new wave of "three strikes and you're out" laws that resulted in far more convictions leading to life sentences. These and other initiatives led to the uniquely American practice of incarcerating even juveniles for life without parole. Harsh policies on parole eligibility for lifers were adopted by many parole boards, legislative bodies, and governors, thus increasing time served in prison before granting parole.

The New Generation of Harsh Sentencing Policies

The punitive turn in criminal justice beginning in the 1980s was dominated by a series of sweeping "tough on crime" sentencing laws designed to send more people to prison for longer periods of time. The rhetoric of the time created a bidding war in which political candidates and lawmakers competed to endorse ever harsher sentencing policies. Proposed policies would do little to deter crime but contributed considerably to the current record number of life sentences.

A key driving force in the expansion of life sentences has been the proliferation of habitual offender laws. These policies have been in place in American criminal codes since at least the 1920s but expanded rapidly in the 1990s under the guise of three-strikes laws. Now in effect in half the states, these laws typically require a sentence of life imprisonment upon conviction of a third serious or violent crime, or even a second crime in some states.

Rather than exclusively targeting individuals who pose the greatest risk to public safety, habitual offender laws have in many cases widened the net to impose life sentences on those who, though they were convicted of multiple felony crimes, do not require decades-long incapacitation for public safety purposes.

The case of Louisiana lifer Fate Vincent Winslow is an example of the expansion of life sentences through habitual offender statutes. Winslow, an African American man, was sentenced to a life without parole sentence after his fourth nonviolent felony conviction: he was convicted of simple burglary in 1985 and again in 1994, and was convicted a third time for drug possession in 2004. In September 2008 Winslow was arrested for selling twenty dollars' worth of marijuana to an undercover police officer. Homeless and destitute at the time of his crime, Winslow was charged under the state's habitual offender law which carried a sentencing range from twenty years to life without parole. The jury spent less than an hour deliberating before convicting him on a ten-to-two vote. Louisiana is one of just two states that doesn't require a unanimous verdict for conviction, with ten votes being sufficient. The ten votes for conviction were all from white jurors; the two votes for acquittal were from black jurors. Following conviction, the judge sentenced Winslow to life without parole under the habitual offender statute. Winslow is fifty years old and will serve the rest of his natural life in prison. It is perhaps not surprising that Louisiana maintains the nation's highest rate of incarceration.

The expansion of life sentences through habitual offender statutes also comes about through laws that target individuals who commit a series of crimes in close proximity. Consider a person with a substance abuse problem who commits three robberies in the course of a week to support his addiction. Under many state statutes, he can be charged as a habitual offender and face decades in prison.

In some states the implementation of habitual offender laws has had a direct impact on the scale of life imprisonment. Life-sentenced prisoners comprise 24 percent of the state prison population in Alabama, and one of every six (16 percent) of these individuals has been convicted of a nonviolent crime. This is in part attributable to the state's three-strikes law.

Individuals in Alabama are subject to life without parole for non-homicide offenses via the state's Habitual Felony Offender Act, first enacted in 1977 and considered one of the harshest in the nation. Under the law a defendant with three prior felony convictions, violent or nonviolent, could receive such a prison term.

Individuals such as Lydia Diane Jones have been swept up under the law. In 1997, Jones moved out of her home and into her childhood home to care for her terminally ill father. She returned to her home four months later to retrieve items and was arrested. Unbeknownst to her, Jones's former boyfriend had been using her home while she was away to store and sell marijuana. She was convicted of marijuana possession and, because it was her fourth felony, was sentenced to life without parole. Her initial three felonies had resulted from a string of check forgeries seventeen years earlier to buy food for her children. Jones was ultimately exonerated based on demonstration of an inadequate legal defense; in September 2017, she received a full pardon. In part due to cases such as this, the Alabama state legislature amended the law in 2015 to require that the prior convictions all be for specified violent offenses.

States with indeterminate sentencing structures that allow for a greater degree of judicial discretion have also contributed to the expansion of life sentences by extending sentencing ranges up to life imprisonment. Such policies have led to high proportions of life-sentenced prisoners with the possibility of parole in Colorado, Nevada, and Utah.

Utah's sentencing scheme calls for a range of five years to life imprisonment for first-degree felony convictions (which include categories of non-capital murder, sex offenses, and kidnapping). Nearly a third (30 percent) of people in prison in Utah are serving life with the possibility of parole, the highest proportion in the country. The state Board of Pardons and Parole notes on its website that the Board assumes jurisdiction over the individual upon admission, and, "when a person is sent to prison in Utah, the offender must serve the entire sentence imposed, unless the Board acts to release the offender prior to the expiration of the sentence."[1] Though most individuals are considered for parole, the Board has the authority to deny future parole hearings for anyone who appears before them.

Thus, a life *with* parole sentence can be transformed into a life *without* parole sentence.

Mandatory sentencing and habitual offender laws have not been received well by the federal and state judges charged with implementing them. In one review of federal judges' opinions on sentencing, repeated concern was voiced about the long sentences required in certain cases of nonviolent and/or first-time offenses. According to one judge, sentences that held people for nonviolent offenses past the age of sixty were "pointless."[2] Moreover, for those with no likelihood of release before death or old age, some judges are troubled that these individuals will have no hope, and therefore little incentive to be "model prisoners." Federal judges have expressed much frustration about their limited discretion at the sentencing stage in cases where a mandatory life sentence is the required sentence. Individuals who pose little threat of physical harm but have been convicted of three drug offenses can be subject to mandatory life without parole sentences under harsh federal sentencing structures.[3]

Extending Parole Wait Times

The number of people serving indeterminate life sentences has risen as parole boards and legislative bodies have extended the time to be served in prison before parole consideration. This has been accomplished by prolonging both the wait time before an initial parole hearing and the wait time between subsequent hearings.

States such as Michigan have taken cutbacks in parole consideration to extremes. Beginning in 1942, people with parole-eligible life sentences in Michigan could go before the parole board after ten years. In practice, most were released within a few years of becoming eligible. In 1992 a change in state law required a minimum of fifteen years before parole eligibility. In addition, an increasingly conservative political climate led to a position of the parole board that "life means life," and that in order to be released, "something exceptional must occur."[4] This policy contrasted with the understanding of judges when they had imposed life sentences. In a 2002 survey of judges conducted by the Michigan State Bar, a majority responded that the possibility of parole was a factor in their sentencing decisions and that they had assumed that parolable lifers would serve twenty years or less. Data from the Michigan Department of Corrections show that while 124 lifers were paroled in the 1960s, only 31 were paroled in the 1990s (with a far larger prison population than in the 1960s). The Michigan experience is not unusual and shows the power of parole boards to influence the meaning of life sentences.

Similarly, a life sentence with the possibility of parole in Tennessee now requires that a minimum of fifty-one years be served before meeting with the parole board. Tony Baldwin had been convicted of murder in 1979 and sentenced to a life term. At the time of his sentencing, the state's policy was that individuals had to wait thirty years before becoming eligible for parole. But Baldwin's good institutional record had earned him sentence-reduction credits that moved up his hearing to 2001, after serving twenty-two years. His request for release was denied by the parole board, which also told him that he could not apply for release again for twenty more years, until 2021. In a challenge to the decision, the state Court of Appeals ruled in 2003 that the decision represented "an arbitrary exercise of the Parole Board's authority" and failed to recognize that "over time people can change, and that even a convicted felon may be able to live in accordance with the law." The court concluded "the essential effect of the Board's action is to change Mr. Baldwin's sentence to life without parole, contrary to what the Legislature intended."[5]

Other states have extended the minimum term of years to be served before parole consideration as well. For example, a 1994 law in Missouri extended the initial wait time before parole consideration from thirteen years to twenty-three years. In addition, prisoners who had been denied parole previously had to wait two years for a rehearing, but policymakers changed this to five years in 1993.

In Georgia, persons serving life sentences for serious violent felonies committed before 1995 were eligible for parole after seven years. In 1995 the legislature doubled this period to fourteen years. The statute was revised again in 2006, requiring a thirty-year period before initial parole review on a life sentence for persons convicted of any of seven serious, violent felonies: armed robbery, kidnapping, rape, murder, aggravated sodomy, aggravated sexual battery, and aggravated child molestation. In its press release describing the new policy for these "seven deadly sins" offenses, the State Board of Pardons and Paroles boasted, "parole for a life sentence is a rare commodity."[6] In a report on the implementation of the law, the state Department of Corrections noted that "Georgia's 'Seven Deadly Sins' law *is the toughest in the nation.* Not three strikes but two—and the second strike results in life without the possibility of parole" (emphasis in original).[7]

Parole in these cases is seldom granted. Even after serving as much as three decades in prison, only 19 percent of life-sentenced prisoners considered for parole were granted parole in 2014, compared to 44 percent of those serving non-life sentences.[8]

The Declining Use of Clemency for Life Imprisonment

At one time, gubernatorial grants of clemency for relief from a sentence of life without parole were a viable possibility, but the use of this power has declined precipitously in recent decades.[9] In Pennsylvania, for example, a state in which all life sentences preclude the opportunity of parole, the changes have been dramatic. There has been both a steady decline in the number of cases recommended for commutation by the parole board to the governor and a decline in the number of cases approved for clemency. While 251 people were granted clemency (an average of thirty-one per year) between 1971 and 1978, commutations have stayed in the single digits since 1995, even amid a much larger life without parole population.[10]

Some states have eased the ways in which an individual sentenced to life without parole can be released, such as through geriatric or medical parole mechanisms. Virginia and several other states have such a policy, but it is rarely utilized. Between January 2014 and March 2017, Virginia granted geriatric release (eligible for individuals who are at least sixty years old and have served at least ten years in prison) to just 68 of the 1,417 cases reviewed (figures for all eligible sentences, not just life sentences).

Adult Crime, Adult Time

> There is no great joy in sending a young person to prison for life. But it will create a healthy deterrent that people know the rules of the game have changed.[11]
>
> —FORMER FLORIDA GOVERNOR JEB BUSH, 2000

After a period of relative stability in juvenile crime, homicide arrests for youth under the age of eighteen nearly tripled from 1985 to their peak in 1993. In many low-income communities, the rise was even more dramatic. Concerns about violence were widespread, as were concerns about the government's ability to respond effectively. But this concern was amplified by widespread circulation of grossly inaccurate predictions about juvenile violence by a variety of sources—media, policymakers, and opinion leaders. The term "superpredator" was created to describe a new breed of teenagers on the horizon who were predicted to be especially violent and remorseless. Such predictions were soon recognized as highly inaccurate, but they were nonetheless influential in policy development.

American juvenile justice policies underwent a dramatic reversal of direction during the final decade of the twentieth century, including the decision to route increasing numbers of teenagers from the juvenile court system to the adult criminal court system for processing. At both the state and federal levels, juvenile transfer policies were widely endorsed. Once in the adult system, where age-related factors have much less salience and mandatory sentences are common, young people became increasingly vulnerable to life sentences. These accumulated quickly and lasted past the 1993 peak in serious crime. Whereas only nine juveniles were sentenced to life without parole in 1979, by 1996 that figure had mushroomed to 160.

In their zeal to pass juvenile transfer laws, most lawmakers failed to consider the full spectrum of adult sentences to which juveniles would be subjected, the inappropriateness of these sentences given the developmental immaturity of juveniles, and the consequences of mandatory imposition of the sentences. In Pennsylvania, for example, any sixteen- or seventeen-year-old charged with first- or second-degree murder was automatically transferred to adult court and, if convicted, received a mandatory sentence of life without parole. Thus, both in the decision of where to try the case and what sentence to impose, a judge would have no discretion to treat a young teenager differently from an adult who committed the same crime. In most instances the decision to enhance the imposition of life sentences on children was not arrived at through deliberation and debate; instead it came as a secondary consequence of the policies, now widely viewed as misguided, that expanded the number of young people handled in adult court.

The impact of juvenile transfer laws on the life-sentenced population has been considerable. Our data show that in addition to the more than 2,300 individuals who were under eighteen at the time of their crime and were serving life without parole at year-end 2016, 7,346 people in this category were serving parole-eligible life sentences and another 2,089 were serving fifty years or more. Combined, this amounts to well more than ten thousand juveniles, or 6 percent of the total life-sentenced population.

Anita Colon and Robert Holbrook

Anita Colon makes a one-hour daily commute each way to her job as the director of patient financial services for a major Philadelphia-area hospital system. It's a demanding job, but it wasn't always her only one. She was also a mother, a wife, and the sister of one of Pennsylvania's more than 520 "juvenile lifers"—individuals sentenced to spend the remainder of their lives in prison for crimes they committed before the age of eighteen. And the work commute? Not nearly as long as the six-hour drive each way, month after month, year after year, to visit her brother, Robert, in the penitentiary.

"It happened on his sixteenth birthday," Anita said of her brother's crime. "He was a kid, a typical fifteen-year-old boy. Rambunctious, funny, smart, lots of energy. He was caring and giving, more so than many his age." But somewhere, something went wrong.

It wasn't gangs, it wasn't drug use, and Robert was not considered a troublemaker. But, said Anita, in the months leading up to the crime, "he had absolutely begun to hang around with a bad crowd." A local drug dealer began throwing some money around to the neighborhood's younger kids, sending them to the store for a soda with a twenty-dollar bill and letting them keep the change. Robert observed, and then developed a fascination for the flash and fantasy. "It was a seduction," said Anita. "No doubt about it."

They paid him five hundred dollars to be an outside lookout for a drug deal. But it went bad, the wife of a rival dealer was killed, and for his part, without any foreknowledge of events, sixteen-year-old Robert Holbrook was sentenced to life without parole.

That was twenty-seven years ago; a child's decision that changed not only his life but that of his entire family. When the judge spoke the words at Robert's sentencing, "life without parole," the family initially experienced them with a detachment from reality. Robert's mother was devastated. His stepfather kept asking Robert's attorney to explain how much time he would actually serve.

Robert looked to his family, his tether, but found nothing to reassure him that it was all a mistake. From their reaction he knew it was bad. Anita, still in grad school, was no more equipped to unravel the complexities of the criminal justice system than anyone else in the family. Though she knew the sentence for second-degree murder was mandatory life without parole, it wasn't supposed to be that way. Not for Robert, not for a child.

Robert fully cooperated with authorities from the beginning. "We believed that just telling the truth and cooperating was the best thing. My brother went in and willingly gave the whole version of his participation and what happened." Based on his cooperation, the district attorney extracted an "open" plea deal: in exchange for Robert's testimony, the state promised to reduce the charge to third-degree murder which carried a significantly lesser sentence.

Everything seemed to be in place, but the other adult defendant pleaded guilty to first-degree murder to avoid the death penalty in exchange for his testimony and Robert's value fell. The defense attorney had failed to secure a "Boykin" agreement, a written and legally binding plea deal. "He should have gotten a written agreement," Anita said of the attorney. Initially, prosecutors had threatened Robert with the death penalty. Anita understood this to be hardline posturing, but it was no less frightening, nor was it needed. The family, and Robert too, simply did not believe that a sixteen-year-old who did not kill anyone, despite the threats, would be sentenced to life without parole. They presumed the district attorney was acting in good faith when Robert made his "blind" plea. "Did we think there was any chance whatsoever that [life without parole] was the sentence he would receive? Absolutely not. If we had it to do over again, we would not have allowed him to take a general plea."

Not so subtly hidden under the district attorney's betrayal is race. Robert is biracial; his father is African American, his mother Caucasian from Germany, his skin color and hair clearly favoring his father. Race played a factor, of that Anita is certain. "It was just so inherent at that time with the district attorney and the policies of that office," she said. "Without a question, African Americans and Latinos are treated differently and much more often labeled guilty without proper review. As the nation's leader in life without parole sentences for juveniles, Philadelphia County, where Robert was convicted, is responsible for more than 60 percent of all such cases in Pennsylvania.

The sheer callousness of the state's disingenuousness drove the life without parole pronouncement like a twisting knife to the heart of Robert's family. Robert, who was taken from the courtroom and placed into a holding cell with other juveniles adjudicated that day, was struggling to wrap his head around what had just happened. The television in the cell was showing cartoons, Anita remembers Robert telling her some time later, and, instead of thinking, he just watched the images. "He couldn't comprehend it. Like many in his situation, it was just too much to take in."

It was the beginning of her brother's journey, though at the time Anita had no idea that it would lead her to become one of the most influential and knowledgeable juvenile justice reform advocates in the country.

For nearly fourteen years, Anita's mother made regular trips to prison. She also wrote Robert every day. "Sometimes it was just a postcard, sometimes a long letter," Anita said. "But she wrote without fail. That was her child and she wanted him to know she was always there." The letters continued until they just couldn't, a couple of months prior to her death. Knowing she was dying, Anita's mother extracted a promise from her—that she would continue to visit and maintain regular contact with Robert, and that she would never stop fighting for his release.

When Robert and Anita's mother passed away in 2004, just months before the U.S. Supreme Court's decision in *Roper v. Simmons* that eliminated the death penalty for juveniles, a decision that would become the catalyst for future rulings about how the justice system treats juveniles, Anita picked up where her mother left off.

Through the Pennsylvania Prison Society, a nonprofit prison reform advocacy organization, she helped form a juvenile life without parole subcommittee. A short time later she was leading the organization, serving as president of its board of directors. When the national Campaign for Fair Sentencing for Youth was formed in Washington, DC, one of its first tasks was to look at states with juvenile life without parole. Pennsylvania's high numbers made it a primary target, and Anita's name was one of the first to be put forward. She became the campaign's first state coordinator. Today, she travels the country advocating for youth justice reform.

"The most frustrating part of the work is that legislators don't understand the laws they make." She also works with victim organizations. "I think one of the toughest is dealing with victim advocate groups. It is the advocacy groups, not the victims themselves. . . . It is the ones who claim to be the voice of the victims, often just only using them as pawns. But from my experience, they sometimes increase [victims'] pain as opposed to providing comfort or healing."

When *Miller v. Alabama* was decided in 2012, it was one of the happiest days of Anita's life. In *Miller*, the U.S. Supreme Court invalidated mandatory life without parole in homicide cases for juveniles. "I was thinking that this changes everything. Which it ultimately did, but it wasn't until four years later when there was a legal avenue." Lacking clear directives to the contrary, many states, including Pennsylvania, did not apply the ruling retroactively and thus refused to qualify juveniles sentenced before the ruling as eligible for sentencing review. Then, in 2016, the U.S. Supreme Court ruled in *Montgomery v. Louisiana* that *Miller* must apply retroactively.

"The [Pennsylvania] legislature had no plans to do something for Robert and others like him," said Anita. "Each of the pre-*Miller* cases are being handled individually by judges. We've been having many resentencings since *Montgomery*; however there is nothing, no law, no legislative guidance that dictates how the individuals should be resentenced. Life without parole is still on the table."

Robert Holbrook was resentenced on October 23, 2017. His sentencing judge wrote a letter of support saying that, had discretion been an option, he would never have sentenced Robert to life without parole for his role in the crime. Because of Anita's advocacy, and because Robert himself became a model prisoner who earned a degree in higher education and was instrumental in starting college-level programs inside the prison, he was resentenced to twenty-seven years to life. This made him immediately eligible for parole. At the resentencing hearing, Anita would not allow herself to fully believe until she heard the words. "I cannot take it for granted even though I know it is pretty much set," she said just weeks before the hearing. "We have been burned before."

Anita says she has tried to imagine what life had been like for Robert growing up in prison. "Prison is not the normal place to grow up. But I looked at him like I look at my own son or any boy that has grown up into a man. A silly boy suddenly becomes serious. My advocacy gives me some insight, but there is no way to know exactly what it is like. When we were with my brother in the visiting room, he wanted to be with family, not bring prison into the visiting room."

Anita credits Robert for educating her about the issues. "Most of what I know about juvenile life without parole I learned from him," she said. "He did the research in the beginning, contacting advocacy organizations and sending me information." Anita, bound by family and a promise, did the rest.

Robert had his parole hearing on January 18, 2018, and was granted parole one week later. On February 20, 2018, Robert Holbrook was released from his life sentence to return home to his family and begin his new life at the age of forty-three.

Doing Life

The ways in which people serving life terms cope with their incarceration should be an important consideration for policymakers, correctional staff, and the public. Policies that facilitate effective and inclusive programming contribute to higher prisoner and staff morale, a more efficient use of resources, and reductions in recidivism. Policies that work against these objectives aggravate prison overcrowding and heighten tensions within institutions.

Prison is an artificial environment that shares few commonalities with the outside world. A range of facility and individual characteristics influence the prison experience, including staff conduct, physical design of the prison, program and education availability, and classification level of the institution.[1] These features are all beyond the control of incarcerated individuals. Nevertheless, they must learn to navigate them to "succeed" in prison. And though individuals learn to cope with living in prison, this environment is very different from the outside world; the coping skills gained in prison are not easily adaptable to society and in some ways are counterproductive.

The gap between life in prison and life in society is partially attributable to policy shifts of the past few decades that have prioritized incapacitation over developing the vocational, educational, and social skills necessary for crime-free reintegration. Whereas people with life terms were once able to work toward meaningful correctional privileges like attaining trusty status or off-site furloughs, and whereas prison programming focused to a greater extent on preparing individuals for successful reentry, regressive crime policies have substantially restricted these options. Some correctional policies prioritize participation in programming for those with an upcoming release date, which places those serving life at an extreme disadvantage. Even if a prisoner is eligible, programs frequently have long wait-lists, and those with life terms are at the back of the line. Ultimately, for those serving life sentences, accessing programs can frequently mean a years-long wait.

Declining Opportunities for Programming in Prison

Opportunities for earning meaningful privileges were not always as limited as they are in prisons today. Prison furloughs, for instance, were used extensively between 1950 and the late 1980s. These practices typically allowed eligible prisoners to travel outside the prison walls to attend to a family emergency or funeral, or to visit family to preserve relationships. The furlough experience is recounted by one person serving life as something that "gave you some incentive to do the right thing."[2] Today these motivating programs are largely absent or have been severely restricted.

Furloughs faced major criticism in the wake of the notorious crimes committed by Massachusetts prisoner Willie Horton in 1987. While out on a weekend furlough twelve years into his life sentence, Horton failed to return to prison. Ten months later he committed an assault, robbery, and rape in a home in southern Maryland. His crime became a major issue in the 1988 presidential campaign because of then presidential candidate Michael Dukakis's expressed support of the state's furlough program.

At the time furlough programs were in place in all fifty states. Prisoners serving life without parole for first-degree murder could particulate in furlough programs in thirty-seven states, as well as in the federal system. One study of the Massachusetts furlough program examined recidivism among nearly two thousand released prisoners in 1973 and 1974 based on whether the prisoner had participated in a furlough program prior to release. The results showed a 16 percent recidivism rate for furloughed prisoners compared to a 27 percent recidivism rate for non-furloughed prisoners in 1973, and a 16 percent recidivism rate among furloughed prisoners in 1974 compared to a 31 percent recidivism rate for non-furloughed prisoners in 1974.[3] Though Horton's crimes were tragic, this experience was an extreme aberration; a sixteen-year evaluation of the program showed that the Massachusetts furlough program maintained a success rate (defined as a voluntary return from a furlough) of 99.5 percent.[4]

Policies that reserve rehabilitation and education programming as rewards contingent on good behavior overlook the benefits that would be derived for both the individual and the prison environment if programming were available to prisoners who are more challenging to manage. In many western nations, programming is the central component of the prison experience, the underlying philosophy of this approach being that it is the function of the institution to reform the individual.

Even for a well-adjusted prisoner, a life sentence is an impediment to accessing self-improvement programs. Criminologist Timothy Flanagan notes that "for most of the history of institutional corrections, correctional policymakers put long-term prisoners at the bottom of the list of priorities."[5] A 2012 study by The Sentencing Project surveyed 1,579 individuals sentenced as juveniles to life without parole to learn about their backgrounds and experiences in confinement.[6] We found that 62 percent of respondents were not engaged in rehabilitation or educational programming, with a third reporting being excluded from participation because of their life sentence. Another 29 percent reported that they were housed in prisons without sufficient programming to allow them to participate, or that they had already completed all the programs that were offered.

Corrections officials frequently justify excluding people serving life sentences from participating in programming under the rationale that limited resources require the institutions to prioritize services for those who are nearing release.[7] Another contention is that the seriousness of the crime committed means that these individuals are incapable of change.[8] This bias exists despite evidence of low reoffending rates among individuals released from a life sentence. Consider the following account by a life-sentenced prisoner from Washington:

> A lifer, even though it seems like on paper he doesn't have anything to lose, he's got a lot to lose because of what he's trying to achieve in the facility that he's in. He's trying to do the right thing, make the right choices, stay with family [on extended family visits], programming. All these things, which would be ruined immediately if he were to act out. They're the most stable. They're the best card to play. The staff here know that. They know that most lifers don't get into any trouble at all. Very seldom.[9]

Transformations in Prison

A considerable body of research examines how individuals cope with living in prison.[10] Acclimation to the prison environment as well as to the reality of a life sentence causes enormous strain, and it can take years before the import of a life sentence is fully appreciated, especially in the case of teenagers. Loss of freedom, an uncertain future, a high degree of personal insecurity, and losing authority over daily life decisions constitute the "pains of imprisonment."[11]

Individuals arriving at prison on a life sentence are in an extremely vulnerable state, both emotionally and physically. Adjusting to prison is difficult for all, but far more so for those who recognize they may never leave the prison.[12]

Studies on disciplinary actions taken against lifers over time show that while infractions are likely to accrue at the beginning of a sentence, they taper off with time as many lifers mature and become positively engaged in their environment. Ethnographic accounts show that they come to view prison as their home, "an involuntary one, to be sure—but still a domestic world in which they have an investment; they care about such things as the level of cleanliness, the quality of the food, the variety of activities, and even relations with their keepers."[13] Moreover, many lifers view their prison environment as all they have left to control in life and thus attempt to make the most of it: "they obey the rules and generally stay out of trouble, secure good jobs, and generally fill their days with structured activities—all so that they might live fully in the present and give as little thought as possible to the world they left behind."[14]

Almost all (95 percent) of the respondents to our survey of juvenile life without parole prisoners reported disciplinary actions taken against them at some point, typically for misbehaviors such as disobeying orders, possessing contraband, failing a drug test, or altercations with other prisoners. But the rate of this misconduct declined over time. The volume of disciplinary reports showed that of those who had been in prison for less than ten years, only 19 percent had not had a disciplinary report in the past three years. Among those who had been in prison ten years or longer, the number without an infraction rose to one-third. And for those who had been imprisoned for more than thirty years, nearly two-thirds had been incident-free for at least the past three years. These findings suggest that misbehavior dissipates with time spent in prison, and this can occur well before a life sentence typically expires.

Many lifers engage in work, pursue educational goals, and participate in spiritual and rehabilitative programming when they have the opportunity to do so. But the opportunities for formal programming are typically less available. The Corrections Court Reentry Program at Angola prison in Louisiana provides one means of allowing life-sentenced prisoners to demonstrate their reformation. The program pairs short-term prisoners convicted of a nonviolent offense with life-sentenced prisoners at Angola. The life-sentenced prisoners provide vocational training after they themselves have become certified in a wide range of vocational skills. The program has had initial success in lowering recidivism among short-term prisoners who are released.

Prison officials who are strapped for resources may have little incentive to spend them on those who may never be released. Yet excluding this segment of the prison population from programming raises two concerns. First, the diminishing opportunity for prison programming means that individuals have little to show for their personal reformation when they appear before parole boards for review. At the individual level, this reduces chances for a favorable parole outcome, as participation in prison programming is understood to help prepare individuals for success outside prison. At the aggregate level, this has contributed to the buildup of life-sentenced prisoners, as new cases are added on the front end and fewer are released on the back end.

Criminologists Lila Kazemian and Jeremy Travis note that, because of the extended length of stay in prison, people serving life sentences can be assets to the prison environment through their leadership and mentorship capacity.[15] Because lifers are excluded from the larger society and family relations are strained by the separation (and perhaps because of the separation), many seek to build meaningful social bonds within the prison. Mentoring younger prisoners is a common way of finding meaning for people serving life; this meets an inherent human need for connection and also fosters the emergence of a new identity as a positive influence on others.[16]

Ethnographic studies of lifers over the long term reveal that they increasingly avoid interpersonal conflicts that might erupt into violence. For some, this is part of the natural "aging out" that occurs as individuals mature, whether they are incarcerated or not. Maintaining a stabilizing, predictable, and peaceful environment emerges as a central goal of life-sentenced individuals. Nevertheless, a record of institutional misconduct, even if only at the beginning of the sentence, may significantly reduce the odds for eventual parole for those otherwise eligible.

Relationships with the Outside World

A recurring theme in the personal stories of long-termers is that they face challenges that those with shorter sentences do not experience to the same degree. Maintaining relationships with others in the outside world is chief among these, which affects not only the individuals in prison but their families as well. Only half of all parents in prison maintain contact with their children through calls and letters, and less than one quarter do so through in-person visits. These rates drop with longer prison sentences.

Long prison sentences are especially straining on romantic partnerships.[17] Dutch criminologist Marieke Liem's documentation of the experience of life imprisonment reveals that some in prison find it preferable to terminate relationships that would otherwise impose a burden on family and friends of sustaining the relationship through visits, mail, and phone calls.

Vulnerable Populations

Women sentenced to life imprisonment have elevated psychosocial needs and greater suicidal tendencies than men. They also report more experiences of childhood abuse, including sexual abuse, and higher rates of intimate partner victimization.[18] These forms of trauma are more pronounced for life-sentenced women than for women serving lesser, non-life sentences. While the lifer population is typically viewed as a male group, the fact that the pace of growth for women serving life has been more rapid than for men suggests the importance of reevaluating their status in these institutions.

As we have documented, nearly 12,000 people currently serving life sentences were under eighteen at the time of their crime, representing 6 percent of all life-sentenced individuals. The physical, social, and emotional limitations of young people create special challenges when they arrive in adult prison. Data from 2010 show that half of these individuals were still under eighteen at the time of their conviction; of these, nearly one-quarter were immediately placed in the general population of an adult prison from the start of their sentence. Such an environment allows no protections for young age or physical vulnerability. To address this, corrections officials sometimes use solitary confinement with the goal of reducing occurrences of assaults on these youth. While such placements may have some effect on safety, solitary confinement can also be particularly harmful for younger individuals.

The widespread use of solitary confinement is a growing concern within the context of mass incarceration. While it is sometimes imposed for serious infractions such as gang involvement or escape attempts, the majority of lifers interviewed in Marieke Liem's study attributed their time in solitary to "nonviolent breaches of prison rules."[19] In its 2014 comprehensive assessment of the growth of incarceration, the National Research Council reported that mental health declines while incarcerated can be attributed in part to chronic prison overcrowding and the growing use of solitary confinement.[20] The mental health needs of people serving life sentences are more pronounced than for others,[21] and these are exacerbated during isolation.

The fiscal cost of life imprisonment is high, in the range of $1 million per adult in prison, with expenses rising precipitously after middle-age.[22] A key component of the doubling of expenses as prisoners age is the heavy toll that prison itself has on an individual's health. Typically, people entering incarceration already exhibit poorer health compared to the general population, but the harsh prison environment, accompanied by inadequate treatment, exacerbates prisoners' health status and accelerates the aging process. People in prison experience higher rates of both chronic and infectious diseases as compared to the general population.

Coming Home

Even with the personal transformations that often occur in prison, life-sentenced individuals face obstacles beyond their control in their quest to gain parole release. Parole boards are usually politically appointed, and their decisions are tethered to the executive office. If a paroled prisoner commits a serious crime, the governor is frequently blamed because of his or her role in approving the board members, even though paroled lifers generally have low rates of recidivism. Consider the outcome of paroled Massachusetts prisoner Dominic Cinelli, who had been serving life in Massachusetts. On his release in 2010, Cinelli killed a police officer during a department store robbery. In response, the governor terminated five of the seven parole board members. The parole grant rate for people serving life sentences dropped precipitously. Some life-sentenced prisoners who were approved for release and were in transition facilities but had not yet been formally discharged were called back to continue their prison sentences. The political consequences from a tragic outcome like the Cinelli case reduce the odds of release for others.

Reoffending rates for people who have served a life sentence and been paroled are considerably lower than for the general population in prison. Based on this observation, one might conclude that imprisonment "worked." But a closer look at the experiences of these released individuals suggests otherwise. The dedicated conformity to prison rules and social order makes for a "model prisoner," but not necessarily for a person competent to manage life outside, where choice and autonomy are key considerations. Significantly, Liem found that those most likely to succeed on parole had developed considerable self-efficacy; their conformity in prison was the product of choice rather than blind obedience. As a result, they were better prepared for the outside world, though the obstacles awaiting them in the free world were formidable.

As individuals leave prison they confront a largely hostile or indifferent world. Bruce Western's extensive work documents the profoundly negative effects of long-term incarceration on employment prospects, income, and social ties. Rather than empowering individuals to be self-supporting, prison itself generally leads to a greater reliance on public assistance. Released lifers and other long-termers struggle with homelessness, joblessness, and irreparable breaks in social ties. They face ostracism because of their time in prison. Because decades have passed, they must quickly catch up on technological developments that have transpired during their imprisonment. One released lifer described his lack of preparation for the changed world into which he was released as having been "placed in a foreign country."[23]

When individuals leave prison, many if not most report feelings of extreme anxiety, stigmatization, and isolation.[24] These are signs of the "institutionalization" brought about by decades-long exposure to the prison setting.[25] Studies of long-term prisoners show that these individuals exhibit attitudes and behaviors associated with heightened levels of post-traumatic stress disorder (PTSD), serious obstacles to assimilation into society, which differs radically from prison life. Researchers have identified a "specific cluster" of mental health problems among released lifers, including signs of institutionalized personality characteristics, lack of trust in others, difficulty forming relationships, and social-sensory disorientation such as spatial disorientation.[26]

Rather than providing robust rehabilitation programming, many institutions have made cuts to programming due to either fiscal constraints or the political environment. This approach routinely fails to prepare individuals adequately for release, which would be challenging even in the best of mental health conditions. Nevertheless, those who return to prison—for lifers, it is usually on a technical violation rather than a new offense—are portrayed as engaging in a "willful and deliberate refusal" to conform to society's norms and laws.[27]

"Death Is Different"

The growth of life imprisonment sentences in recent decades draws an inevitable comparison with use of the death penalty in the United States. In both cases the United States is unique among democratic nations in maintaining and imposing such severe levels of punishment. To the extent that life without parole is often viewed as an alternative to a death sentence, questions of policy, practice, and human rights arise.

The growing legal understanding that "death is different" provides a certain level of protection and consideration for the unique role that the death penalty plays in the criminal justice system. This understanding, though, is more often an aspirational goal than a practical reality, given the abysmal scale of funding for high-quality criminal defense, limitations on appellate review, and the sordid nature of the execution process itself. The deficiencies of the death penalty process should raise serious concerns about sentences of life imprisonment, which receive far less scrutiny.

Legal decisions that support the idea that "death is different" essentially imply that life imprisonment is not "different." This plays out in a host of ways that disadvantage those facing such sentences. It means that there are fewer resources devoted to defending people facing a life sentence, such as funds for expert witnesses, as well as more limited ability to have cases heard by appellate courts following conviction. There is also less public scrutiny of the court process itself in life imprisonment cases. It is now not unusual to hear reports of individuals having their death sentences overturned as a result of DNA evidence or witnesses recanting their testimony at trial, whereas the ability to achieve these results is far more difficult in life imprisonment cases due to the resource limitations.

The Death Penalty in the Courts

The Supreme Court has drawn a sharp distinction between the death penalty and all other criminal sentences, with respect to the Eighth Amendment consideration of what constitutes "cruel and unusual" punishment. Through a series of rulings, the Court has clearly concluded that "death is different." Beginning with *Furman v. Georgia* in 1972, which halted executions due to their being imposed in an "arbitrary and capricious" manner, the Court has found that "the penalty of death differs from all other forms of punishment not in degree but in kind."[1] This distinctive view of death sentences as qualitatively different from non-death sentences has lasted through a series of jurisprudential challenges.

Four years after *Furman*, the Court marked the beginning of the modern death penalty era in *Gregg v. Georgia*.[2] After reviewing Georgia's new law, which established separate trial phases for determination of guilt and sentencing, the Court allowed states to reinstate the death penalty through a system of guided discretion.

On the same day the justices delivered their ruling in *Gregg*, they also issued an opinion in the case of *Woodson v. North Carolina*.[3] In this instance, they ruled that death could not be imposed as a mandatory sentence, because such a process would not allow for consideration of a defendant's individual characteristics. The justification for this specialized level of consideration was that a death sentence was "qualitatively different from a sentence of imprisonment, however long." The Court emphasized the importance of considering "more than the particular acts by which the crime was committed" in deciding whether to impose the death penalty.

Finally, the Court noted that "in capital cases the fundamental respect for humanity underlying the Eighth Amendment requires consideration of the character and record of the particular offense as a constitutionally indispensable part of the process of inflicting the penalty of death." Essentially, a death sentence requires a higher standard of review and accuracy because of the permanency of the punishment.

In a series of rulings since then, the Court's approach to "cruel and unusual" challenges has supported categorical bans on imposing the death penalty: specifically, it is no longer legal in the United States to impose the death penalty for crimes committed by juveniles or by persons with mental retardation or for crimes other than capital murder. Nonetheless, the Court still upholds the death penalty for a range of situations, well into the twenty-first century, long after most western nations have endorsed abolition.

Life Imprisonment Is Not "Different"

The logical inference of the Supreme Court's findings that "death is different" is that all sentences less than death *can* be held to a lower level of scrutiny. This is precisely what has played out with regard to life imprisonment, in the realms of both legal challenges and public policy. We can see the consequences of these decisions both in lower court rulings regarding excessive sentencing and in the level of scrutiny and resources applied to litigation regarding life sentences generally.

Cruel and Unusual Considerations in the Courts

The Supreme Court has been reluctant to find that life imprisonment is excessive. In the Texas case of *Rummel v. Estelle*, decided in 1980, the Court considered the case of a man sentenced to life with parole for a third offense of felony theft.[4] Had the prosecutor charged the defendant with a single offense rather than as a habitual offender, the sentencing range would have been between two and ten years. Instead, with two prior fraud crimes (amounting to a combined total of about $230) being included in the charge on conviction, William James Rummel received a life sentence. The Supreme Court held that the conviction did not constitute cruel and unusual punishment, noting that "the state had a significant interest in dealing in a harsher manner with those who by repeated criminal acts have shown that they are simply incapable of conforming to the norms of society."[5]

A decade after *Rummel* the Court addressed extreme sentencing for drug offenses in the case of *Harmelin v. Michigan*.[6] Ronald Harmelin, a defendant with no prior criminal record, was convicted of drug possession under Michigan's "650 Lifer Law," referring to the quantity of drugs in grams that would trigger a life without parole penalty. Harmelin was sentenced to life based on the large amount of drugs found in his possession (672 grams of cocaine), a discovery made during a routine traffic stop. Harmelin's attorneys argued that the sentence was disproportionate to the crime, but the justices ruled that severe, mandatory penalties were not uncommon and thus did not constitute cruel and unusual punishment. The justices also opined that Harmelin's sentence was not without hope for release, as he might qualify for executive clemency.

By 1998 more than two hundred individuals in Michigan had been sentenced to life without parole under the 650 Lifer Law, enacted in 1973. More than 86 percent of these people had not been previously imprisoned. With public opinion increasingly opposed to the policy, the Michigan legislature reformed the law in 1998 to allow parole eligibility. On the occasion of the repeal, former Republican governor William G. Milliken called his original signing of the law "the worst mistake of my career."[7]

Despite Michigan's policy shift, the Supreme Court's draconian approach to life without parole was cemented further in a 2003 challenge to California's three-strikes law. Gary Ewing was convicted of the theft of three golf clubs but, based on his long record of prior offenses, received a sentence of twenty-five years to life.[8] Leandro Andrade's third strike was for theft of $153 worth of videotapes from a Kmart store, for which he was sentenced to fifty years to life. Ewing and Andrade argued that their sentences constituted cruel and unusual punishment, but the Court found no constitutional issue with the state's penalty structure and deferred to the state legislature to make determinations on criminal sentencing. In her opinion for the Court, Justice Sandra Day O'Connor wrote that, just as in *Rummel*, the sentence was based on "rational legislative judgment" which is "justified by the state's public-safety interest in incapacitating and deterring recidivist felons."

The key exception to these rulings is the case of *Solem v. Helm*, decided in 1983.[9] In this instance the Court held that a mandatory sentence of life without parole was unconstitutional for a South Dakota man convicted of a seventh nonviolent felony offense. The Court based its decision on the view that the crime was a petty criminal act and thus the mandatory life sentence was disproportionate.

A more recent alternative view of life without parole as worthy of Eighth Amendment analysis comes from Justice Sonia Sotomayor's concurring opinion accompanying the ruling in *Campbell v. Ohio*.[10] Glen Campbell, convicted of aggravated murder and sentenced to life with no opportunity for parole, appealed his sentence on unrelated grounds, but Justice Sotomayor used the ruling to convey her uneasiness with life sentences "not subject to review," as is the case in Ohio. She noted that "a statute that shields itself from judicial scrutiny of sentences of life without the possibility of parole raises serious constitutional concerns." Relying on the trilogy of juvenile cases which pointed out the permanency of a life sentence along with the grave responsibility of the sentencer, as well as the language from *Gregg v. Georgia* that emphasized the uniqueness of the death sentence, Justice Sotomayor invited consideration of "other sentencing practices in the life-without-parole context to ensure that they were not imposed arbitrarily or irrationally."

A Lesser Level of Scrutiny for Life Imprisonment

The conclusion that "death is different" has led to less scrutiny of life imprisonment sentences, even though they are frequently imposed through mandatory sentencing policies and share many of the qualities of death sentences.

In addition to restrictions placed on the death penalty due to juvenile status and mental retardation, heightened safeguards in case review and appeal distinguish death sentences from other sentences. In capital cases attorneys often receive specialized litigation training. And while procedural errors and claims of substandard representation occur regularly, these claims at least have an established process for review. Capital defendants also have the right to state-appointed counsel for the appeals process, in contrast to non-capital defendants.[11] And though appeals are usually possible in non-death cases, these are frequently time-barred, and certainly more so than in death-eligible cases.

Even with the stringent regulations that have been crafted around the death penalty, errors are rampant. Since 1972, 161 death row prisoners have won innocence claims, including 27 in Florida alone. Substandard legal counsel is all-too-prevalent in death penalty representation, and mishaps in executions arguably amount to torture. If this is how punishment is carried out with enhanced layers of scrutiny, one can only imagine the miscarriages of justice that take place for individuals serving life sentences.

For life sentencing cases, court procedures are far more limited and no specialized training is provided to defend or prosecute such cases. Moreover, the lack of heightened review in life sentencing cases brings an increased likelihood that innocent individuals will be convicted. The number of individuals exonerated after receiving a sentence of life without parole—frequently perceived as an alternative to the death penalty—is not known, but it is likely to be far higher than the figure of 161 in death penalty sentences. This is the case both because the number of people serving a life without parole sentence is far higher than for death sentences and because there is much less scrutiny of life without parole sentences.

For example, in 1992, three eight-year-old boys were murdered, and their bodies were discovered the following day in a muddy river in West Memphis, Arkansas. Teenage defendants Jessie Misskelley, Jason Baldwin, and Damien Echols were tried and convicted for the murders despite documented concerns about preservation of the crime scene, the interrogation, police records, and the trial. Misskelley received life with parole, Baldwin life without parole, and the eldest defendant, Echols, was sentenced to death. It was only because the case received prominent national attention by investigative journalists and Hollywood celebrities that the state ultimately revisited the case. An appeal to the State Supreme Court in 2007 revealed that the state did not have conclusive DNA evidence that placed the three at the scene of the crime. Eventually, all three sentences were vacated, and the men, now known as "the West Memphis Three," were released after serving eighteen years in prison.

Juveniles *Are* Different

Supreme Court consideration of life without parole sentences for juveniles represents the only area in which the death penalty is *not* "different" from other sentences. The Court first took up the question of cruel and unusual punishment in 2009 while considering the constitutionality of a life without parole sentence for seventeen-year-old Terrance Graham's armed burglary conviction.[12] Graham was one of 109 individuals around the country who had been sentenced to life without parole for a non-homicide offense, 77 of which originated in Florida.[13] The Court, relying on adolescent development science, ruled that, because of juveniles' stage of development, the decision to permanently exclude them from society was, at a minimum, premature. Juveniles are different from adults in at least three critical ways, the Court reasoned: they are more likely to take risks, less able to extricate themselves from peer pressures (especially negative ones), and less able to foresee the consequences of their actions and feel remorse for them. These features are a natural part of adolescence, and as individuals develop into adulthood, these age-specific characteristics fall away. To sentence an individual to life without parole for a non-homicide offense before they have fully developed is a violation of the Eighth Amendment, the Court ruled.

In 2012, the Supreme Court again took up the issue of parole-ineligible life sentences for juveniles in *Miller v. Alabama*, which considered the constitutionality of life without parole sentences for juveniles when imposed under a mandatory sentencing structure. At the time, such statutes were in place in twenty-nine states and the federal government and accounted for approximately 2,000 of the 2,500 individuals nationwide serving these prison terms. Among states with mandatory sentences following a murder conviction, the rise in juvenile life without parole sentences imposed in the previous three decades was three times greater than in states that allowed judges to impose lesser sentences.

The plaintiff in *Miller v. Alabama*, Evan Miller, was fourteen years old at the time of his crime. Together with an older co-defendant, Miller committed an arson in which the inhabitant died, a crime punishable by a mandatory term of life without parole regardless of the perpetrator's age.

Mandatory life without parole for a juvenile precludes consideration of chronological age and its hallmark features. It prevents taking into account the family and home environment that surrounds him—and from which he cannot usually extricate himself—no matter how brutal or dysfunctional. It neglects the

circumstances of the offense, including the extent of his participation in the conduct and the way familial and peer pressures may
have affected him.

In its decision, the Court barred mandatory life without parole
for juveniles, again relying on their demonstrated lack of maturity and the lesser criminal culpability that accompanies youth.
In Justice Elena Kagan's opinion for the Court, she outlined the
age-related factors that could mitigate culpability but that were
prohibited from consideration under the mandatory sentencing
structure. The so-called "Kagan factors," which are now required,
include not only the child's age at the time of the offense, but
an appreciation of adolescents' maturity level, tendencies toward
impetuosity, and common failure to evaluate risks that go with a
young age. In addition, the court should consider the child's home
and family environment; the circumstances of the offense, including the role taken and the pressure exerted by others; the child's
lack of sophistication relative to an adult; and the possibility for
rehabilitation.

Research on the lives of juveniles serving sentences of life without parole supports the claim that children who commit violence
are often victims of neglect and abuse. In Miller's case, for example, both parents were addicted to crack cocaine and it was, in fact,
his mother's drug dealer whose house he burned down, killing him
in the process. Miller had also attempted suicide multiple times in
his short life, the first time at the age of six.

In the years following *Miller v. Alabama*, state courts offered con-
flicting interpretations as to whether the ruling should apply retroactively to the two thousand individuals serving these sentences.
The Nebraska Supreme Court, for instance, ruled that the twenty-
seven individuals serving juvenile life without parole at the time of
the *Miller* ruling should have their sentences reviewed in light of
the ruling.[14] Luigi Grayer was one of the beneficiaries of this ruling. At age fifteen, Grayer committed a homicide—the result of a

botched purse-snatching—and was sentenced to life in prison with no opportunity for parole. At sixty years old, he had served forty-five years in prison, had suffered a stroke while incarcerated, and required the use of a wheelchair. He was granted a new sentence in the aftermath of the *Miller* ruling that allowed his release in December 2015.

Yet in states such as Pennsylvania, the ruling was interpreted as prospective only. Pennsylvania is by far the country's leader in incarcerating people serving these sentences, currently more than five hundred. Because Pennsylvania decided not to apply *Miller* retroactively, Trina Garnett, who was fourteen at the time she tragically killed two people, remains in prison forty years later.[15] Homeless and mentally disabled, by age fourteen Garnett had endured abuse and neglect for years. Though serious doubts about her ability to stand trial were raised, she was tried and sentenced as an adult, and given life without parole under the state's relatively unique statute requiring mandatory life without parole for first- *and* second-degree murder convictions. The Pennsylvania Supreme Court's resistance to applying *Miller* retroactively to people convicted as juveniles before 2012 would have meant that Garnett would die in prison but for a third Supreme Court case.

In 2016, the U.S. Supreme Court resolved states' contradictory application of *Miller* in *Montgomery v. Louisiana*, ruling that states must apply *Miller* retroactively.[16] Without the *Montgomery* ruling, the opportunity for parole release would have continued to be afforded in some states but not in others, perpetuating a system of justice by geography. Each of the affected states, including Pennsylvania, is now in the process of revising their approach to juvenile life without parole sentences, through either the parole process, legislative remedies, or individual resentencing. Though life-in-prison sentences are still an option (including life without the possibility of parole), all the affected individuals now qualify for a review of their original sentence with consideration of age-related factors.

The Slow Decline of the Death Penalty

Campaigns to eliminate the death penalty in the United States have made significant advances in recent years, to the point that death sentences have now been outlawed in nineteen states and the District of Columbia. Even in states that still allow it, most apply it only rarely. Nonetheless, the United States remains in the company of nations including China, Iran, Saudi Arabia, and Iraq in carrying out executions and is the only western democracy to do so.[17]

With public support for the death penalty declining and a growing number of prosecutors losing their zeal for executions, there is reason to believe that the practice could be discontinued in the coming years, through either litigation or practical obstacles to its retention. Challenges to the death penalty have focused on the striking numbers of cases of innocence, the arguably torturous methods of execution, and the staggering expense of capital litigation and appeals. The disproportionate allocation of court resources to death cases has come at the expense of both civil litigation and scrutiny of non-capital criminal sentences.[18]

The decline, or eventual abolition, of the death penalty will place issues of life imprisonment in greater focus, as that becomes the harshest penalty in the American court system and as life without parole sentences continue to be employed as a legislative strategy to abolish the death penalty. How the lessons learned from the experience with the death penalty translate to considerations of life imprisonment will help to define the scale of punishment that our society views as reasonable and fair.

Sam Lewis

Labeled by teachers as disruptive and angry, an emotionally lost sixteen-year-old Sam Lewis was easily lured into the violent culture of mid-1980s Los Angeles gangs. His descent into the miasma began with the turbulent breakup of his parents' marriage—Sam began internalizing his anger and could not communicate his feelings to his mother, family, or teachers. Sam found father figures through gang life. The gang's violent culture became his path to feeling accepted. "The more violent you were, the more acceptance you got," he recalled. "They were great negative mentors." At age eighteen, Sam was convicted of a gang-related killing and sentenced to fifteen years to life.

Thirty years later, the adult Sam is an affable, competent, educated, and focused man who serves as director of inside programs for the California-based Anti-Recidivism Coalition (ARC), a nonprofit that works to prepare prisoners for life after incarceration and advocates for criminal justice reform. "It's a very long way from there to here," he said, recalling his pivotal moment about ten years into his sentence. It was during a visit with his seven-year-old daughter. "I knew she was coming to visit on the weekend, but I got into an incident on the Thursday before and was sent to administrative lockdown. She had never seen me in shackles and chains and behind the glass. She asked me, 'Daddy, why can't I hug you?' I tried to explain that I had gotten in trouble, but realized there was no good answer."

Sam's daughter made one request of him, to try to stay out of trouble so that when she returned she could hug her dad. It was just five words, "Why can't I hug you?" but they shook Sam to his core. "I didn't know how I was going to change, but I knew at that moment I wanted to change."

It didn't happen overnight. After getting out of "the hole," he restarted his participation in the prison's Alternative to Violence Program, classes he had once used only as a way to get out of his cell. This time he put in the work, internalizing the teachings and tools. In time he became a certified facilitator. Seeking even higher ground, he earned his GED, then enrolled in correspondence courses. Sam then decided to do something about the dearth of educational and life-skills programs offered by the California Department of Corrections and Rehabilitation. He petitioned the department to allow the creation of self-help organizations, called Inmate Leisure Time Activity Groups. Today, these programs are ubiquitous throughout California's system including Alcoholics Anonymous and Narcotics Anonymous, Veterans in Prison, Victim Offender Education Groups, and PRIDE—Prisoners Reaching Independent Decision to Educate. It was not a straight path. Gangs hold significant sway in California prisons, and Sam's efforts, perceived as a challenge to their influence, generated resistance. But Sam understood gang culture and used that insight to develop a community of prisoners who found common ground in the desire to build a different life.

Sam continued his education, earning an associate degree in paralegal studies. He helped other prisoners to file writs, appeals, and civil legal documents, a skill that would take him through the gauntlet of parole review. Despite stacking up impressive credentials, Sam was denied parole eight times. After the seventh denial, he filed a writ with a state appellate court claiming that the process lacked a rubric and denial was arbitrary. The court agreed and remanded his case to the parole board to specify reasons for denial. On his ninth attempt, the board saw it his way, and he was released in 2012 after serving twenty-four years.

The former gang member, convicted killer, and lost soul makes no excuses. He knows both the pot-holed path that led to prison and the six years since, during which he has translated the hard-earned insight, integrity, maturity, leadership, and life skills into a career vocation that advocates for those he left behind.

Walking out of Soledad Central Prison, Sam could hear shouts from the windows of the cell blocks, most pleading with him to represent those who work consistently for redemption. He wears their faith in him like a favorite coat. "I don't promote myself as the exception to the rule because I'm not," he said. "There are others like me who want to do good things and give back, so I try not to allow anyone to exceptionalize me."

Time in prison is often time stood still for family left behind. Being released can mean taking those relationships off pause. Everyone had different expectations of Sam; he had his own. He worked hard to stay focused and do what he needed to do. Released at age forty-two without a work history, it was imperative that he prove himself worthy and earn the respect of his family, potential employers, and anyone else who intersected with his life.

First, Sam made it his job to find a job. Each day he began his search at the computer, on the phone, or face to face, attacking the task with a deep-seated need to validate all that he had experienced, learned, and achieved in prison. But as with nearly all formerly incarcerated individuals, Sam's "record" was more than a metaphorical ball and chain. There were many "no"s and rejections in the days and weeks that followed. Finally, he landed a job with Petco, the pet supply company. It was a part-time sales associate position, one he took seriously. He was willing to do anything—arrive early and work late—to prove his worth. It was a work ethic that earned him a promotion offer, but more importantly it carried over into everything that came next.

Soon after, he was offered an unpaid youth mentoring internship through Pasadena's Shields for Families, a nonprofit that provides a range of services for underserved children. It was an invaluable training ground. That internship led to another, paid, position with Friends Outside–Los Angeles County, as a job development case manager. Brick by brick, Sam built upon each opportunity. His life changed significantly when, five years ago, ARC co-founder Scott Budnick brought Sam to a local jail where Budnick was a volunteer mentor. That developed into an offer to join ARC, and now Sam manages a team of specialists and advocates that crisscross California into prisons, communities, and government hallways to prepare prisoners for life after incarceration, create partnerships for jobs, housing, and other services, and lobby for legislation that promotes public safety by reducing recidivism.

Sam particularly credits Budnick, and ARC's Christine Collins, for believing in people who have been incarcerated and giving them an opportunity not only to plug into resources but to lead. "I haven't met very many people who have that kind and level of belief in [formerly incarcerated people] as those two."

A normal Sam Lewis day now begins around 3:15 a.m. He and his wife make a 70-mile commute into the city, where she drops him off at a gym near the ARC offices before heading to her job. He gets in his daily workout and arrives to work around 7 a.m. to go over his schedule. There is some routine, like reviewing daily reports from his Hope and Redemption Team, who travel to prisons around the state facilitating programs, teaching life skills like developing good decision-making processes, and readying inmates for release. He also sets up mentoring programs, attends meetings, and works on reform legislation. Weekends are mostly for family, but for two hours on most Saturday evenings he goes to a local juvenile hall to mentor teenagers who are facing lengthy sentences. Sam's life is a balance of work, advocacy, volunteerism, and family, normal and yet extraordinary in his commitment to give back. He is reminded during the mentoring sessions, as he listens to the stories of the fifteen-, sixteen-, seventeen-, and eighteen-year-olds, where he came from and the path that brought him to redemption. He refuses to give up on them because he remembers too well those who wrote him off such a long time ago.

"I think that anyone who is incarcerated should take this to heart. If you want to be the best at what you do, if you don't know it you need to learn it. If you don't know how to learn it, ask someone to teach you. If you want to be depended upon then be dependable. Be consistent, put in the extra effort, and in the long term it will pay off. That's my personal belief."

Being a former lifer is not something you can always hide from people, nor does Sam want to. "With strangers I meet, in the appropriate setting, I share my story. I tell them about being a teenager and that I take responsibility for my actions. As an adult, I express my deepest sorrow about anything I did to harm anyone. Now I am trying to change the dynamics of gangs, incarceration, prison, and all the things I helped build up to be negative. If I can change one life, at least when I am called to meet my maker I can say I helped change one life."

Sam counters skepticism and cynicism with sincerity and empathy. "If I met a person who has been incarcerated for a gang-related murder I would be doubtful. So, I have to show them. I can show them better than I can tell them. I am thankful for the supporters who believe in me because it allows me to continue to move forward and make a difference."

He is most proud of coming home and showing his mother that her faith in him was justified. "That's the greatest thing, knowing her belief in me was well founded. She never bailed on me, she always encouraged me, and being able to come home and show her she was right is what I am most proud of."

The daughter who engineered his change is now an adult recently returned to the Los Angeles area. Five whispered words, louder than she would ever have imagined, created the catalyst for change not only in one man, but through him change in the lives of hundreds. Sam Lewis, former gang member turned difference maker, lives like the man he knows he was created to be.

The American Commitment
to Punishment

In 2016 fifty-five-year-old Susan Gwynne was arrested by police officers for a string of burglaries and thefts in Delaware County, Ohio. Gwynne had been employed as a nurse's aide in a number of senior living facilities, and video surveillance identified her as entering patient rooms and coming out with a bulging handbag. Upon obtaining a search warrant for her home, officers found more than three thousand stolen items, including jewelry, credit cards, family photos, military medals, and other mementos.

Following plea negotiations Gwynne pleaded guilty to a mix of forty-six felonies and misdemeanors. She had no previous felony convictions and just a minor misdemeanor record. At her plea hearing Gwynne claimed that her thefts were done to support her cocaine addiction.

At sentencing the prosecution recommended a prison term of forty-two years, while the defense argued for intensive community supervision and a period of time in a community-based corrections facility. After considering the applicable sentencing statutes, the sentencing judge imposed varying sentences of six months to three years for each of the forty-six charges, but to be served consecutively, not concurrently. As a result Susan Gwynne was sentenced to sixty-five years in prison, a "virtual life" sentence, making her eligible for release at the age of 120.

Upon appeal the Court of Appeals ruled that the sentence of sixty-five years was "plainly excessive" and amounted to a life sentence. The judges noted that the sentence was "an emotional response to very serious and reprehensible conduct" but did not comply with the purposes of sentencing. The Court modified the sentence and concluded that fifteen years was "consistent with the purposes of sentencing." So, without any prior felony convictions, Susan Gwynne's spree of burglaries and thefts will now keep her imprisoned until the age of seventy.[1] Her sentence is but one of many that illustrate the extremes to which American punishment policy has evolved, laying the groundwork for the massive imposition of life sentences.

Life Sentences in an Era of Mass Incarceration

Fully understanding how such an extreme number of Americans came to be serving life sentences requires exploring the contours of the punishment state, which is remarkable and unprecedented in the history of democratic nations. Despite modest declines in the U.S. prison population in recent years, the rate of incarceration is first in the world.[2] The political and cultural assumptions that have produced these outcomes made the massive expansion of life sentences virtually inevitable.

Why and how the world's wealthiest nation, and one with a long tradition of struggles for democracy, could come to embrace mass incarceration is a challenging question. We know a great deal about the proximate causes of these developments—mandatory sentencing policies, enhanced drug law enforcement, cutbacks in parole release, and other shifts in policy and practice. We also know that since 1980 the rise in incarceration has been *entirely* produced by changes in policy, not crime rates.[3] But this still does not tell us *why* the United States came to embrace such a direction.

The Historical Foundations of Mass Incarceration

In the past several decades historians and legal scholars have explored these issues from a variety of perspectives. Explanations for the enhanced commitment to punishment in the United States include: class distinctions determining levels of punishment; the ongoing legacy of racism; structural differences among nations in how public policy is developed; and the political impact of the 1970s shift in emerging globalization and its consequences for the American economy.

James Q. Whitman's exploration of the nature of punishment in the United States compared to France and Germany takes us back to the origins of incarceration in the eighteenth century. These European nations had two forms of punishment: a restrained maintenance of dignity for high-status offenders and "degraded" treatment for commoners. In contrast, in the relatively egalitarian American social structure, both high- and low-status offenders were subject to harsh treatment. Over time, as class distinctions in these European nations diminished, European punishment was "leveled up" and the lower-class prisoners were afforded the treatment previously reserved for the aristocracy, while the U.S. punishment regime remained unchanged.[4]

The dramatic growth in American inequality since the early 1970s tracks precisely with the growth of mass incarceration. This has had implications both for the underlying contributing factors for crime and for the orientation of public safety policy. Anthony Doob and Cheryl Marie Webster examine the relationship between high incarceration rates and societal values, such as minimum wage policies. They point to a body of research that demonstrates that nations with low rates of economic disparity and generous social welfare policies also generally maintain low imprisonment rates.[5]

By the late twentieth century elements of political grandstanding and racist imagery came together in the formation of criminal justice policy. Few observers would say the choice to feature Willie Horton, a black man, as the poster child for harsher punishment during George H.W. Bush's 1988 presidential campaign was coincidental. Indeed, on his deathbed, Lee Atwater, Bush's campaign manager, apologized for the "naked cruelty" of the attack on Dukakis.[6] Critics such as the Reverend Jesse Jackson described the ad campaign as racist, and many believed it to be a critical factor in Bush's electoral victory.

The adoption of California's infamous three-strikes policy in 1994 illustrates the impact of media sensationalism on the evolving political environment. The proposal, modeled on a similar measure that had been adopted in Washington State, required a sentence of twenty-five years to life imprisonment for a third felony conviction following two prior serious or violent offenses as defined by the statute. The initiative gained traction following the tragic kidnapping and killing of twelve-year-old Polly Klaas, who was abducted from her home by Richard Allen Davis, a man with a lengthy criminal record who committed the crime while on parole.[7]

In the zeal to pass a harsh statute to prevent such crimes in the future, campaign organizers established that the third "triggering" felony could be violation of any such statute in the state. Out of this grew outlandish distortions of sentencing policy which, as previously noted, were not found to be unconstitutional by the U.S. Supreme Court.

Despite this fundamental shift, a number of states and the federal government have established sentencing guidelines commissions to avoid these irrational outcomes. The commission structure typically consists of a body of experts, including judges, law professors, and others in the legal community, isolated from the legislative process and therefore free to make rational choices about sentencing policy. While the commissions have achieved some measure of success, legislators in most jurisdictions have adopted mandatory sentencing policies that trump the guidelines structure developed by the commissions. As a result, prison populations have expanded across the board in the United States, in states both with and without sentencing commissions.

Racism as a Driving Force in Mass Incarceration

One cannot assess the dynamics of incarceration in the United States without tracing the impact of racism. This is not to claim that the United States is unique in this regard. Broad racial disparities can also be found among indigenous populations in Canada, aboriginal people in Australia, and the Maori population in New Zealand.[8] But the unprecedented scale of mass incarceration in the United States means that in absolute terms racial disparities translate into mind-boggling numbers of African Americans whose lives are profoundly affected by sentencing policies, including life imprisonment.

The penitentiary system in the United States developed in contrast to the colonial practice of placing offenders in the stocks or banishing them from the community. Believing those practices to be unduly cruel, reformers created the penal system that originated in Philadelphia in the early nineteenth century, premised on helping "sinners" become "penitent" through Bible study, often with the aid of outside readers coming into the prison cells. An alternative model was later pioneered at Auburn Prison in upstate New York, employing a work regimen under a code of silence, so as to prevent the "convicts" from communally planning future crimes.[9] Neither of these models proved terribly effective in reforming the sinners and convicts, nor did they lead to any serious reflection on the goals or structure of the penitentiary system.

While the current situation is historically unique, the intersection of race and criminal justice is longstanding and has taken on a variety of forms over several centuries. At the inception of the penitentiary system, many of the confined population, especially in the

South, were white citizens who broke the law. In southern states, there was a sharp transformation of the prison system after the Civil War. Prior to the war, prisons were filled almost exclusively by whites because most African Americans in the region were enslaved. But after the abolition of slavery new means developed to exploit black labor.

Under the ingenious system of "convict labor," newly freed African Americans were arrested and charged with a variety of offenses, often for discretionary and suspect violations such as vagrancy.[10] Following a quick conviction and sentencing, state authorities would then lease out the labor of the new "convicts" to local landowners and business leaders using the clause of the Thirteenth Amendment that permitted forced labor for those convicted of crimes. In many cases this new form of black labor was eerily parallel to the enslaved black labor of previous decades and frequently performed on the same plantations where African Americans had been enslaved.

In *Slavery by Another Name*, Douglas Blackmon notes that, while the system of convict labor "was a form of bondage distinctly different from that of the antebellum South," it was "nonetheless slavery—a system in which armies of free men, guilty of no crimes and entitled by law to freedom, were compelled to labor without compensation, were repeatedly bought and sold, and were forced to do the bidding of white masters through the regular application of extraordinary physical coercion."[11] Blackmon shows that these labor substitution schemes were not a short-term reaction to the loss of black labor in 1865 but persisted through the early decades of the twentieth century, in both southern and northern states.

While perhaps not as extreme in its impact as the convict labor system, there are modern-day versions of law enforcement strategies that embrace its dynamics. Just in the past decade, two strategies have received widespread attention that, despite their ostensible goal of enhancing public safety, have consciously targeted low-income communities of color for heavy-handed policing with no societal gains.

The "stop-and-frisk" strategy of street-level police engagement has been employed in many cities and has been the focus of major litigation and political battles in New York City. Originally begun in the 1990s as an element of "broken windows" policing, the program involved massive numbers of street stops—reaching as high as six hundred thousand annually—with the vast majority taking place in black and Latino communities.[12] The policy served little public safety purpose: only a very small proportion of the stops led to an arrest for possession of drugs or weapons. But the collateral damage of the initiative was substantial, as young men and women in these communities increasingly felt that the police were not their protectors but agents of oppression.

Following a years-long court challenge, in 2013 a federal judge ruled the stop-and-frisk practice unconstitutional.[13] As a result, the number of stops plummeted by more than 90 percent in the following years. Despite police officials warning of a crime spike if the practice was ended, crime rates continued to decline in New York City, including in the formerly targeted communities.

A second policing strategy in the national spotlight is the targeted enforcement of low-level violations as a means of generating income for local jurisdictions. Not until the aftermath of the Michael Brown killing in Ferguson, Missouri, did the nation learn how widespread this practice had become. A major assessment conducted by the Department of Justice laid out the strategy in graphic detail.

Political leaders in Ferguson, a small suburban community with a limited tax base, faced challenges in how to support their schools, roads, law enforcement, and other vital services. Their solution was to conduct massive numbers of street stops by police, disproportionately targeting the town's black population. The stops included such incidents as pedestrian infractions and minor automobile safety violations, all of which resulted in high fines and fees assessed by local courts. For those who did not have the resources to pay the fees (and in the absence of any inquiry by the courts regarding ability to pay), jail terms became a frequent penalty. Judges would then frequently negotiate with jailed citizens about payment plans to gain release from incarceration. It soon became clear that these practices were not unique to Ferguson, as journalistic accounts and stories emerging in class-action litigation demonstrated the widespread nature of this discriminating policing strategy.

The Development of Mass Incarceration

By the mid-1960s, crime rates began to rise in the United States. Though lawmakers seeking to gain political advantage exaggerated the increase, it was nonetheless real and substantial. This is most clearly seen with murder, the offense with the highest rate of reporting. These rates nearly doubled from 5.0 per 100,000 in 1960 to 9.8 by 1974. Other crimes most likely were rising as well, though crime data for that period was far less comprehensive and rigorously reported than today.

In retrospect, we know a good deal about the origins of rising crime rates during this period. Most prominently, there was the coming of age of the "baby boom" generation, the large cohort of children born in the postwar decade after 1945. As any parent knows, teenagers engage in misbehaviors and crimes at elevated rates, though this is a period that generally lasts only a few years. As this group came to constitute an increasing portion of the general population it should not have been surprising that a crime spike might develop.

Other factors were influential as well. The United States was becoming a more urbanized society in the postwar years, and urbanization is frequently associated with higher rates of crime due to increased day-to-day stress, greater exposure of young people to peer groups at the expense of family, and the lure of consumer goods, among other factors. The ripple effects of social inequality may have contributed significantly as well. Criminologist Elliott Currie points to the disproportionate effect of rising unemployment among nonwhite youth as "sufficient to explain increasing crime rates for youth."[14]

The emerging crime problem became linked with emotionally charged national debates about the civil rights movement and the Vietnam War. Richard Nixon's 1968 presidential campaign famously highlighted the problem of "crime in the streets," which was in part a reflection of rising crime but was also conflated with the growing conservative hostility to the civil rights and antiwar movements.

These years marked the beginning of crime being elevated as a national concern. Prior to this, crime had largely been addressed as a local issue, unless there was a high-profile crime such as a celebrity murder. But the lethal mix of rising crime rates and the widening chasm of American opinion on social policy, racism, and cultural styles created fertile ground for some opportunistic leaders to transform crime into a "wedge issue" that could be employed to enhance political power.

To note these developments is not to suggest that the problem of crime and violence was just a distraction manufactured by politicians, for indeed the problem was becoming more serious by the late 1960s. How to address this problem, though, was a politically contested battle, one that not only shaped criminal justice policy but also exacerbated the growing political divide in the country.

Coincident with the coming shift in criminal justice policy was an emerging new conservative movement, represented by the presidential campaigns of Republicans Barry Goldwater in 1964 and Richard Nixon in 1968 and 1972. Building on the public divide over the Vietnam War and the civil rights movement, these campaigns sought to portray an aggrieved (white) American working class—as typified by the "hardhats" in the construction trade—as the "real" Americans who worked hard and were strong patriots, in contrast to what President Ronald Reagan would later describe as the (black) "welfare queen" who allegedly was receiving overly generous welfare payments and living a life of luxury.

As criminal justice policy began to shift in the 1970s, it did so along with a changing political environment on immigration, social welfare policy, and other divisive issues. The period also marked the beginnings of the well-documented skewing of income and wealth in the United States, as rising globalization, the oil crisis of 1973, and the decline of manufacturing took a heavy toll on communities of color in particular. The need for industrial labor had opened up union-wage jobs for both blacks and whites in the auto and steel industries, and the civil rights movement had begun to break down barriers to opportunity, but now urban communities were hit hard economically and began to be perceived as a "surplus" population.

Policymakers of the 1970s responded to the growing problems of rising crime rates, drug use, and drug selling with a strong commitment to criminal justice approaches and enhanced punishment. Yet such a response to crime has not always been an accepted principle nor is it the norm in many communities today. Achieving public safety is a complex undertaking that is not primarily premised on the threat or use of punishment.

Parents understand this, and those in the middle and upper classes have the resources with which to establish strategies that are not reliant on punishment. They seek out good schools for their kids, find health professionals to provide quality medical services, and expose their children to a range of cultural, athletic, and educational opportunities. They don't describe these actions as "crime control," but essentially that's one of their hoped-for outcomes. By creating opportunities for their children, they reduce the prospects for well-off children to engage with the criminal justice system.

This is not to suggest that middle-class and upper-class children are immune to criminal activity; in fact it is well documented that they engage in similar levels of misbehavior and criminal activity as do all teenagers. But, more often than not, their families use the resources at their disposal to bail them out of trouble and give them the "second chance" that too many low-income children never receive.

Public safety can best be conceptualized as the outcome of various social institutions and policies. For communities with resources, the preferred focus is on prevention and treatment, with the justice system and its punishment orientation as a last resort (as we now see with the primarily white opioid crisis). But in the era of mass incarceration, the response has been reversed, with criminal justice the policy of choice, particularly for low-income communities and communities of color.

The goal of reducing the scale of life imprisonment will require both policy initiatives to change sentencing standards and a cultural shift in thinking about how to produce public safety. Elements of such a change have emerged in recent decades, including restorative justice, bail funds to prevent pre-trial incarceration, reentry programs, community policing, and a variety of treatment-oriented court systems. For now we acknowledge the challenge before us, and we will explore how to advance these changes later.

The Meaning of Life
Around the World

Hope is an important and constitutive aspect of the human person. Those who commit the most abhorrent and egregious of acts and who inflict untold suffering upon others, nevertheless retain their fundamental humanity and carry within themselves the capacity to change. . . . To deny them the experience of hope would be to deny a fundamental aspect of their humanity and, to do that, would be degrading.[1]

—JUDGE POWER-FORDE, CONCURRING OPINION IN
VINTER AND OTHERS V. UNITED KINGDOM (2013)

The scale of punishment overall, and the uniqueness of life imprisonment in particular in the United States, can be seen most dramatically in comparison with other industrialized nations. The United States locks up its citizens at five to ten times the rate of Canada and western European nations.[2] A portion of this difference can be explained by the higher rate of violence in the United States, and in particular a homicide rate (even following the substantial decline since the mid-1990s) more than five times that of nations such as Austria, Switzerland, Spain, and the Netherlands.[3] The high homicide rate in the United States, in turn, can be attributed in substantial part to the ready availability of firearms. It is, after all, much easier to kill someone with a gun than with a knife, sticks, or your hands. Even taking these differing rates of violence into account, less than half of the combined prison and jail population in the United States is confined for a violent offense. Persons sentenced to prison in the United States generally receive longer prison terms than for comparable crimes in other nations.

The contrast in the imposition of life sentences can be seen in the context of a key decision by the European Court of Human Rights in 2013. In the case of *Vinter and Others v. United Kingdom*, the Court essentially barred the imposition of life without parole sentences in member nations. Based on the principle that all prisoners should have the "right to hope," the decision requires that individuals who have transformed themselves in prison and have atoned for the harm they have caused should be considered for release at some point in their prison term.[4]

The Vinter case is noteworthy because of the nature of the crimes. All three plaintiffs had committed murders described variously as grotesque, sadistic, and torturous. In one case, young children were killed; in another, four men were killed in part because of their sexual orientation. In Vinter's case, he had already been released twice before from prison for serious crimes before committing his third serious offense. Despite the severity of these crimes, even these individuals were deemed by the European Court to be capable of reform.

Limitations on the imposition of life sentences can be seen in other nations as well. Few crimes in the Netherlands are subject to life imprisonment; instead, the law provides for imprisonment up to twenty years and/or a fine.[5] A review of Dutch sentencing policy by law professor Peter J. Tak demonstrates how a strong commitment to non-institutional sentences produces a lesser level of punitiveness across the board. The Financial Penalties Act of 1983, calling for fines rather than incarceration and originally intended to be imposed for infractions and minor offenses, by 2000 had become the most frequently imposed penalty for all crimes.[6] The Act also requires judges to provide a rationale whenever they impose a custodial sentence over a fine. Other distinctive features of sentencing policy include the prohibition of consecutive sentences when a defendant is charged with multiple crimes. Instead, a concurrent sentence may be imposed, with the possibility of the sentence being one-third higher than the maximum penalty for a single offense.

Similarly, in Germany, corrections policy is focused on resocialization and rehabilitation, as enshrined in law. The Prison Act of 2008 defines the purpose of incarceration as preparing individuals "in future to lead a life of social responsibility without committing criminal offences."[7] Prison life should approximate as much as possible general living conditions and prisoners are to be engaged in drawing up a treatment program designed to meet their needs. In regard to life sentences, the German Federal Constitutional Court permits such sentences, but they are considered constitutional only if "the prisoner was given a realistic and legally-based opportunity to be released."[8] Few people sentenced to life serve their full sentence. In most such cases individuals are considered for release after serving fifteen years if they are good candidates for successful reintegration into the community.

Persons in custody in German prisons who are viewed as risks for public safety can be held under a provision of preventive detention; about five hundred people were in this category as of 2015.[9] The focus of the detention policy is to prepare individuals for release. As such there are individualized therapy programs and teams of psychologists, and prison officials who make an annual determination of each individual's suitability for transfer to the community. If not approved for release, prisoners may still qualify for a family visit furlough.

In a 2015 study tour of German prisons organized by the Prison Law Office and the Vera Institute of Justice, journalist Maurice Chammah described the conditions of prisoners in preventive detention: one such individual had a room "decked out with teddy bears for when his granddaughter visits, vaguely gothic art on the walls, and a massive window looking out onto a grove of trees."[10]

Conditions for those in this system are oriented toward rehabilitation. Chammah notes that men in the system "are able to roam the grounds of their unit freely from six in the morning until 9:30 at night. They even have a bright blue basketball court."

The Nordic countries as well provide a model for a more rational approach to sentencing for serious offenses. Norway abolished life sentences in 1981, with the government proposal stating that "life imprisonment is not compatible with our conception of humanity."[11] In Denmark and Finland "lifers" can be released after twelve years of imprisonment and, in Sweden, after eighteen years.

It is not only European nations that reject the imposition of life sentences. In Latin America only six of nineteen nations maintain statutes that permit life imprisonment, though in many jurisdictions prison terms can be so lengthy that they constitute *de facto* life terms.[12] There is also the practice of the International Criminal Court, which tries cases of war crimes, genocide, and crimes against humanity. The Court has no provision for sentences of life without parole, and for those cases in which a life sentence is imposed there is a requirement for review after twenty-five years.[13] In 2016, a unanimous decision of the Constitutional Court in Zimbabwe ruled that life without parole constituted cruel and unusual punishment and that the absence of hope for relief would "unnecessarily aggravate and dehumanize the delivery of corrective justice."[14]

The Driving Forces of Punishment in the United States

While the zeal to punish has been a distinguishing feature of the criminal justice system in the United States, research by the Urban Institute demonstrates that this has been exacerbated in recent decades, particularly for individuals with long sentences. In an analysis of time served in prison in forty-four states with complete data between 2000 and 2014, researchers found that prison terms had increased in every state, with the sharpest increases taking place among people convicted of a violent offense.[15]

The determination of sentence length is hardly an outgrowth of a rational scientific process. If it were, then policymakers would be consulting research findings on issues such as the relationship between time served in prison and recidivism, whether prisons are "criminogenic" and make individuals more likely to offend or whether people are more likely to desist from crime after going to prison versus being sentenced to community supervision.

However, this is rarely the case. Instead, political calls for addressing the "crime of the month," often triggered by a high-profile crime, not surprisingly produce bizarre outcomes. Widespread three-strikes policies relied on the rules of baseball instead of criminological research. Favored juvenile crime control strategies included rhyming catchphrases such as "adult crime, adult time" rather than turning to the undeniable evidence that juveniles are not simply little adults, whether or not they commit crime.

By the twentieth century, structural distinctions in how public policy was developed further distinguished the political process in the United States from other countries. Much of this is related to what Julian Roberts and others describe as "penal populism," or the distortions of rational policy produced through ill-informed and politically calculated campaigns.[16]

In contrast, the policy development process in nations such as Germany is largely governed by practitioners within the justice system, based on evidence and dialogue, and in an environment largely shielded from political pressures. Unlike other countries, penal populism in the United States has often produced extreme outcomes through political campaigns, ballot initiatives, and media sensationalism.

One such example of gut-instinct policymaking was the adoption of the notorious 100-to-1 drug quantity disparity between powder and crack cocaine offenses in the federal mandatory minimum penalties established in 1986. Those penalties called for a mandatory minimum sentence of five years in prison for sale of 500 grams (a little over a pound) of powder cocaine, but the same five-year term for sale of just five grams of crack cocaine. At the time there was little discussion in Congress about various ways to deal with the newly formed drug markets or of the appropriate mix of prevention, treatment, and punishment that would be the most effective response to the growing crack problem. Instead, the mandatory penalties were enacted with support from both sides of the aisle. More than 80 percent of the individuals prosecuted under this law have been African American.

Not every policymaking body is solely engaged in political grandstanding. Indeed, the growing momentum for sentencing reform in recent years is based at least in part on an examination of sentencing patterns and effectiveness. But most often there has been little engagement between policymakers and the academic community on these issues, and little has been learned from decades of research.

There is even more of a gap in the failure to examine sentencing and corrections structures in other nations. One might think that this would be extremely fertile territory to explore, given that other industrialized nations have maintained rates of incarceration that are just a fraction of those in the United States without experiencing the spike in crime that many prison proponents would predict.

A key insight of the comparative research on sentencing structures among nations is that they are essentially culturally and politically determined and reflect a society's commitment to punishment. Campaigns to adopt three-strikes policies or to impose the death penalty on drug distributors do not take into account research on deterrence, declining recidivism rates with age, or the cost of long-term incarceration, but rather these responses are typically motivated by political expediency.

Perhaps the most consequential aspect of American sentencing policy for life imprisonment is the impact of a prior criminal record on sentencing severity. Sentencing scholar Michael Tonry notes that this effect became most pronounced beginning in the 1980s, as states and the federal government adopted determinate sentencing structures of various kinds that incorporated substantial increases in punishment for repeat offenses. The shift involved, first, the development of sentencing guidelines structures, subsequently followed by the adoption of mandatory sentencing laws and three-strikes laws. As in the case of California's three-strikes law, a third strike would automatically lead to a sentence of twenty-five years to life, even if the current offense itself would normally be subject to much less imprisonment on its own.[17]

Tonry notes that while these sentencing enhancements are often considered intuitively obvious in the American court system, "the United States is alone among western countries in how prior convictions are handled."[18] To the extent that prior convictions are incorporated at sentencing in other nations, their impact is generally quite modest. In England, for example, increased sentences for repeat offenses are brought to bear only if the prior convictions are "recent" and "relevant" to the current conviction.

Thus, the scale of life sentences in the United States is essentially an outgrowth of the greater zeal for punishment in comparison with other nations. As we have detailed, this can be seen at the top of the scale of punishment with nearly three thousand people awaiting execution on death row, followed close behind by the more than two hundred thousand people serving some form of life sentence. The vast body of research on the death penalty has failed to demonstrate a deterrent effect (though scholars have not conclusively demonstrated its lack of effect either), nor is there convincing evidence that life imprisonment serves as an effective deterrent to crime in a system where penalties are already harsh.

Human Rights Norms and Life Imprisonment

In addition to producing diminishing returns for public safety, excessive prison sentences in the United States fundamentally conflict with international norms and policies of respected national legal bodies. In addition to the *Vinter* decision of the European Court of Human Rights, other judicial bodies have weighed in on the critical need to respect human rights when imposing punishment. In 1977, a decision by the German Federal Constitutional Court focused on the circumstances under which life sentences could be considered constitutional. Relying on the concept of human dignity, the Court required that the prospect of eventual release from prison needed to be incorporated into the sentencing structure and ruled that prisoners needed to have an opportunity for self-advancement during their incarceration.[19]

Within the United States, the American Bar Association has long maintained criminal justice standards that call into question many life sentences. On the issue of sentencing severity, the ABA calls for legislative bodies to "ensure that maximum authorized levels of severity, of sentences and presumptive sentences are consistent with rational, civilized, and humane values. Sentences . . . taking into account the gravity of the offenses, *should be no more severe than necessary* to achieve the societal purposes for which they are authorized" (emphasis added).[20] In 2017, the American Law Institute (ALI) approved its decade-long development of sentencing standards for its Model Penal Code. Its standards line up with the ABA in calling for a length of incarceration that is "no longer than needed to serve the purposes for which it is imposed."[21]

Life and long-term sentences in the United States are not necessarily imposed by vindictive or irrational judges. In many cases judges are required by law to impose life sentences for certain crimes. In addition, most of the people who have been subject to these sentences have committed serious crimes and present a threat to public safety at the time of their sentencing. But it is also the case that other nations, which consider such crimes serious as well, have not chosen to impose such drastic punishments.

Sentences of life without parole, and increasingly life with the possibility of parole, not only result in diminishing returns for public safety but also forego the possibility of personal transformation. In the courtroom on the day of sentencing, no one—judge, prosecutor, defense attorney, or even defendant—can predict how the convicted individual will think and behave in ten or twenty years. Evidence suggests that in many cases reoffending behavior will be much less likely. It is for that reason that competent professionals need to assess an individual's suitability for release at reasonable intervals over time. Such a process should be premised on a determination of public safety objectives but also a vision that provides hope, incentive for personal growth, and, in turn, the opportunity to become a contributing member of the community. In a rational sentencing system, those goals would serve the public interest far better than our current structure.

It is now long past time to reconsider the function and value of the excessive prison terms that govern court systems today, not the least of which are the policies that have combined to produce a prison population with more than two hundred thousand people serving life imprisonment. Lengthy prison terms lead to diminishing returns for public safety and distort how criminal justice resources are allocated. They place a great barrier—growing more extreme each year—on efforts to dismantle the system of mass incarceration. They also deny the possibility of redemption and reconnection to the community for individuals who no longer resemble the much younger lawbreakers who committed a serious crime for which they are incarcerated.

William Underwood

William Underwood with his daughter Ebony.

Growing up in Harlem during the 1960s, William Underwood and his three sisters were raised by a single mother. William's family moved frequently—five times between kindergarten and fifth grade. In addition to being home to a collection of clubs, theaters, and bars where music thrived, Harlem was fast becoming a hotbed for the drug trade. It was in this inner-city brew that William matriculated to the morass of Harlem's drug world.

William began selling marijuana in junior high, learning for the first time in his young life what it was like to have spending money—even a little. He quit school in the tenth grade, still a teen but moving headlong into an adult underworld where the strong often devoured the weak. It was what he knew, but not what he wanted.

By the 1970s, seventeen-year-old William found himself living dual realities—one in the horror and destructiveness of his drug-permeated neighborhood, and the other in the enviably affluent lifestyle of the dealers who were both feared and respected. With demand steady, and some of the "heavy hitters" being charged by the federal and local authorities, a vacuum was created in the trade.

Dealing on the periphery up to this point, William recognized "the opportunity . . . for myself and others I'd grown up with to take pieces of a burgeoning enterprise," he wrote from prison. "It was there, we were there, why shouldn't we?"

Just four days before his seventeenth birthday, William became a father. It changed him. Slowly at first—the ingrained behavior of Harlem street life was not easily undone—then more rapidly and enduringly. Two years after his son, Anthony, was born, William was living "with the woman who would become the mother of my two daughters, Ebony and Miko." Street money was very good, supporting his lifestyle and his family and conferring upon him a status that few kids growing up in Harlem ever have. Street life was not his dream, however. Music was, and through it he began to visualize a better life.

The high school dropout and drug dealer was determined not to be defined by his past or his present. He earned a GED at age twenty-one. About that time, through a friend, he met Van Jay, a disc jockey at New York's premier jazz radio station, and by sheer chance was introduced to the national director of Columbia Records. That bit of serendipity opened a portal for William into the music business and would lead to a lasting friendship. William was also accepted to Columbia University, where he soon met an accountant with whom he would start Cubistic Productions, promoting jazz artists around the city. An express train of success followed, and William was promoting concerts featuring legends including Ray Charles and Milt Jackson. That earned him attention from other major producers and labels such as Atlantic Records. Before long, William was independently promoting artists for top record companies, including Kenny Loggins, Wham!, Earth, Wind & Fire, Rick James, and Kool and the Gang. His release of the album *Steve Arrington's Hall of Fame* produced such seminal hits as "Nobody Can Be You" and "Weak at the Knees," which were later sampled by NWA, Dr. Dre, Ice Cube, 2Pac, Snoop Dogg, and Jay-Z. He rapidly built a reputation as "the" person to see in American music, particularly with black artists.

Little argument can be made about the fact that the profits from his earlier engagement in drug dealing seeded William's rise in the music business. But by the early 1980s, William had developed two priorities: his family and becoming a force in American music. When he wasn't on tour with some of the top musical talent of the time, he was with his children, creating bonds and making memories that would come to sustain and inspire all of them for decades to come.

But on December 6, 1988, federal officials indicted William on multiple counts of conspiracy and running an ongoing criminal enterprise. A year later, following three amendments to the original indictment to include allegations of a criminal enterprise past November 1, 1987, the effective date of the new sentencing guidelines, he was convicted and sentenced to life in prison without parole and a twenty-year concurrent term.

In 1990, William began serving out the remainder of his natural life in federal prison, having been convicted under the 1980s-era RICO criminal enterprise statutes.

His conviction resulted from government testimony alleging that he had engaged in racketeering and supervising a network of drug distribution and related violence. Some of the statutes under which he was convicted required low evidentiary proof of an ongoing criminal enterprise. Those statutes have since been declared unconstitutional and now require that evidence be presented to a jury to be proven beyond a reasonable doubt. This change was not applied retroactively, however, meaning that people convicted of similar offenses today frequently receive lesser punishments.

Thirty years later, William Underwood remains in prison, an individual who has excelled in education, legal, and community service programs and served as a mentor for younger inmates. He earned certification in Microsoft Office and has completed business coursework in import-export and smart investing. William is viewed as a model prisoner, having never had any infractions during his incarceration. His only opportunity for release lies in either Congress passing retroactive sentencing reform or executive clemency. Neither option, in the current political climate, would inspire a man to hope. But hope he does. "I don't believe my sentence is the last word," William wrote. "Born and raised a citizen of the U.S., I've always believed that redemption exists for those that exhibit in their deeds and actions that they deserve it."

His greatest sources of hope, from the beginning, have been his four children, with whom he has maintained a close and devoted relationship, and his three grandchildren, despite being shuffled to and from prisons in Indiana, Georgia, Pennsylvania, Virginia, and New Jersey. "I don't think I could have continued on this path without my children to talk to, laugh and cry with, and just be grateful for each other. This journey has provided insights and perspectives for me that I would have never been able to grasp had this not have happened."

Ebony Underwood, now a rising filmmaker and Soros Justice Fellow, is at the forefront of reform advocacy that centers on the children of incarcerated parents. Her work is personal. Just fourteen when William was arrested, she is determined to somehow win her dad's release. In "Hope for Father's Day," a documentary short she produced about her family, Ebony acknowledges William's past illegal activities but places the onus for his endless incarceration on the failed 1980s War on Drugs with its draconian mandatory sentencing policies. "He wasn't perfect and made mistakes by selling drugs before he had his music career," she said. "What originally was a way out of poverty when he was a teenager, and for so many others, eventually became a one-way ticket to prison." Emoting both passion and pain in the video, Ebony speaks of the love her dad has for their family that "has never faltered throughout the twenty-eight years." She is amazed how he has maintained dignity and a sense of normalcy that has not been diminished over the decades. "The connection we've maintained still bewilders me. Especially when I think about the quarter century we have spent on this journey. My father has remained Daddy. . . . He maintains and strengthens ties with all four of his children."

As previously noted, in the fall of 2014 President Barack Obama announced a clemency initiative for people sentenced under the archaic mandatory sentencing laws. William Underwood's petition described a man with a groundswell of support from entertainers and musicians, religious leaders, reformers, conservatives, sports figures, civil rights leaders, scholars, industry leaders, formerly incarcerated mentees, and more who know and love him—though none so passionately as his children.

By the end of his presidency, Obama granted commutations to 1,715 people convicted of federal drug crimes, including more than five hundred people serving life without parole. William Underwood was not among the fortunate ones.

Neither William Underwood nor his strong network of family and friends view this action as a final decision. William still maintains that the life changes he has made, the interests of justice, and societal compassion provide hope for a more just outcome. He works to make that happen each day.

The Racial Meaning of Life

Among the many troubling aspects of the dramatic scale of life imprisonment in the United States is the broad racial disparity that defines its implementation. Two-thirds of people serving life sentences are people of color. The most dramatic disparity is among African Americans, who constitute nearly half (48 percent) of the lifer population compared to their 13 percent share of the overall population in the country.[1]

As is the case with the composition of the prison population nationally—currently about 35 percent African American—there are some who would say that these disparities may be unfortunate, but they just reflect greater involvement in crime among certain communities of color. But a host of factors beyond criminal activity contribute to disparities both among the general prison population and among lifers. These include socioeconomic disadvantage, the impact of "race neutral" sentencing policies, and race-based perceptions of crime and punishment.

The vast majority of people serving life sentences have been convicted of serious crimes, so there is little doubt that most would be serving a prison term under any circumstances. The question therefore becomes how distinctions are made between those who are sentenced to prison for a finite number of years and those imprisoned for life.

The most substantial body of research on race and the justice system is in regard to the death penalty, in large part because of the extreme nature of that punishment. For three decades scholars have consistently found that race is a critical factor in distinguishing between defendants who are sentenced to death and those who receive a lesser term, generally life without parole. Beginning with landmark research by David Baldus, studies have shown that the race of the *victim* is a key factor in producing disparity. As evidenced in the first major study by Baldus, examining hundreds of cases in Georgia and controlling for a range of variables, regardless of their own race, defendants charged with killing a white person had a four times greater chance of being sentenced to death than those charged with killing a black person.[2]

Rarely, of course, does anyone in the courtroom—prosecutor, judge, juror—state that they seek a death sentence because a white person has been killed, yet these outcomes essentially document that a white life is valued more highly than a black life. It is important to note that not only is there usually an absence of overt racial animus; it may frequently be the case that the practitioners in the courtroom firmly believe they are acting in a manner that is beholden to the facts of the case and not to any characteristic of the victim or defendant. Yet we now know that through the effects of implicit bias and certain structural factors these outcomes are pervasive.

Racial bias in application of the death penalty was challenged most prominently in the 1987 Supreme Court case of *McCleskey v. Kemp*.[3] Warren McCleskey had been convicted of armed robbery and killing a white police officer in Atlanta. There was little doubt about the validity of the conviction, but McCleskey's lawyers argued that the death sentence arose from racial bias in the court system, citing evidence from the Baldus study of race and capital punishment in Georgia. In rejecting McCleskey's claim and upholding his death sentence, the justices did not dispute the research findings but opined that McCleskey had not proven that racial animus was directly involved in his case. Of course, short of a racist comment in the courtroom by the prosecutor, the judge, or a jury member, it would be virtually impossible to make that claim. Since *McCleskey*, numerous similar studies of race and death penalty outcomes have been undertaken in other states, with virtually all reaching similar conclusions to Baldus.

As one means of addressing this problem, legislators in North Carolina adopted the Racial Justice Act in 2009.[4] The Act permitted challenges to death sentences if it could be proven that racially disparate patterns could be identified in the state's capital cases. In fact, this is what subsequently took place. Relying on research by Michael Radelet and Glenn Pierce,[5] Superior Court judge Gregory Weeks overturned three death sentences of black men who had been convicted of killing white men.[6] Frustrated by Judge Weeks's application of the law, Republican legislators and the governor subsequently repealed the law in 2013.[7]

In regard to the impact of race on sentences of life imprisonment, there is much less direct evidence available than is the case with the death penalty. Because the death penalty is literally a matter of life and death, there has been a much greater focus on its implementation. But while there has been less scholarly work on life imprisonment, we can nevertheless trace decision-making patterns that point to the likelihood of similar outcomes.

Evidence of disparate outcomes among juveniles sentenced to life without parole can be seen in a 2012 survey conducted by The Sentencing Project, in which we attempted to test the racial patterns that emerged from the Baldus study. We found that the proportion of African American juveniles serving life without parole for killing a white person—43 percent—was nearly double the rate of African American youth arrested in such circumstances, 23 percent. Conversely, white youth represented 6 percent of those arrested for killing a black person but just 4 percent of those serving life without parole for these offenses.[8] This suggests that African American youth are much more likely to receive life without parole for taking a white person's life than white youth are for taking a black person's life. Racial skewing is apparent among adults as well: for adults in prison, the Urban Institute documents that in thirty-five of the forty-four states they studied, racial disparities in prisons were starkest among people serving the longest 10 percent of terms.[9]

Racially disparate outcomes in life imprisonment cases are likely brought about in part by socioeconomic disparities that overlap with race to create disadvantage in the criminal justice system. Since African Americans have higher rates of concentrated urban poverty and suffer from a substantial wealth gap compared to white Americans, these disadvantages translate into differential criminal justice processing.

Socioeconomic disadvantage begins at the point of arrest. It is now well documented that law enforcement resources are focused disproportionately on low-income communities of color. We have seen this play out in dramatic fashion in police targeting practices in Ferguson, Missouri, and in stop-and-frisk disparities in New York, Philadelphia, and other cities. Overall, the behavior of poor people is generally subject to greater scrutiny than that of well-off residents.

Law enforcement officials often contend that this focus on low-income communities is merely a case of using resources efficiently to go where crime trends lead them. While this is true in part, it is also the case that heavy-handed enforcement persists even when not justified by higher rates of crime. For example, Andrew Gelman and colleagues' research on stop-and-frisk patterns in New York City shows that blacks and Latinos represented the overwhelming proportion of all persons stopped, a pattern that held up both in high-crime and low-crime neighborhoods.[10]

Similarly, Katherine Beckett and colleagues' research in Seattle concludes that police targeting of drug crimes involving crack cocaine resulted in highly disproportionate rates of arrest for African

Americans. This was the case despite the fact that more residents were admitted to public treatment facilities for addictions to heroin than for crack, and that heroin users (who are majority white) engaged in more frequent drug purchases than did crack cocaine users.[11]

Following arrest come the pretrial, charging, and trial stages, where access to resources is critical in understanding differential outcomes for different races. After an arrest, a judge will make a determination about pretrial release, generally based on the judge's assessment of the defendant's likelihood of appearing for trial and risk of rearrest. If the defendant does not meet the formal or informal criteria established by the court, he or she will usually have money bail set. In far too many cases, despite the law saying the ability of the defendant to pay must be a factor, these amounts are set with little consideration of the defendant's ability to pay, which contributes to the situation of more than 60 percent of the population in local jails being detained while awaiting trial, before they have been convicted of anything.[12] There is perhaps no other area of criminal justice decision-making where access to resources determines one's fate in such profound ways.

In addition to pretrial detention frequently leading to job loss and family strain, it also increases the prospects of ultimate conviction and incarceration. This is due in part to a defendant's desire to accept a plea offer in order to settle the case and return to the community, and also because of the difficulty of gathering evidence and meeting with a defense attorney to prepare for trial while incarcerated.

Defendants with financial resources, however, have access to a very different court process, one that can be described as part of a "two-tiered" justice system. In white-collar crime cases—insider trading, embezzlement, large-scale fraud—negotiations between prosecution and defense frequently begin even before an arrest has been made. As financial insiders become aware of a criminal investigation of their actions, they work with their attorneys to seek a settlement of the potential charges while avoiding a formal indictment. This may involve a plea to a lesser charge, payment of a fine, or restitution to victims. If their cases do proceed to trial, their resources allow them to have virtually unlimited access to high-quality legal counsel, sentencing consultants, and expert witnesses, which all too often are unavailable to indigent defendants, who all the while remain incarcerated as a result of being unable to afford money bail.

Impact of "Race Neutral" Sentencing Policies

Life sentences are generally imposed based on a combination of the severity of the defense and a defendant's prior criminal record. The impact of a prior criminal record affects the length of sentence both in states that afford judges a fair amount of discretion and those in which sentencing guidelines or determinate sentencing policies govern the process. These policies include a mix of "habitual offender" laws and mandatory sentencing provisions that generally require a judge to impose the required sentence, whether or not he or she perceives it as effective or reasonable.

The key issue with respect to life sentences is the impact of a prior record on enhancing the severity of sentence. The reason this is critical is that African Americans are considerably more likely to have a prior, or extensive, criminal record than other racial groups. Whether this is due to overly aggressive policing or socioeconomic disparities that translate into higher involvement in crime, the average black defendant appearing in court on the day of sentencing is more likely than the average white defendant to have a prior record.

While this situation has obtained for a long time, in the era of three-strikes laws and similar sentencing policies, the effect of a prior record is magnified to a far greater extent than in previous eras. As we have seen, the California three-strikes policy as originally adopted in 1994 called for a sentence of twenty-five years to life for a third felony conviction, which could be any felony in the state. As a result, ten years after the policy was adopted, nearly half of those serving a three-strikes sentence had a property or drug crime as the current offense.[13]

The racial disparities in the implementation of the law are profound. As of 2016, 29 percent of the state's prison population was African American,[14] while 46 percent of people incarcerated for a third strike were black.[15] Such disparities are virtually inevitable given any type of habitual offender law and contribute to extreme sentences such as those in California.

Racial Perceptions of Crime and Support for Punishment

Furthermore, the fact that African Americans may commit certain crimes more than other racial/ethnic groups does not tell us what the appropriate societal response should be, whether long-term incarceration or some other measure. In making these determinations, we know that sentencing policy is not necessarily conducted in a scientific manner based on research evidence, but rather is very much influenced by racial perceptions.

The key insight in this regard is that whites hold more punitive beliefs than other racial groups. To the extent that whites view certain crimes as "black crimes," their support for harsh punishment increases. We can see this through a number of recent studies.

A 2013 Pew Research Center survey, for example, found that 63 percent of white respondents expressed support for the death penalty, while only 40 percent of African Americans and 36 percent of Latinos supported it.[16] Similarly, a variety of other surveys show greater white support for such policies as three-strikes, trying juveniles as adults, and harsher sentencing in general.

The greater level of support among whites for punishment is

particularly notable in that whites are less likely to be victims of crimes than blacks or Latinos. This is true for both property and violent crimes, and is particularly striking for homicide, where African Americans are six times as likely as whites to be victims.

Public policy attitudes among whites are skewed by the fact that they generally overestimate the proportion of crime committed by African Americans. While people of color commit certain crimes at higher rates than whites, the relative proportions are believed to be even higher by white respondents. For example, a 2010 national survey asking respondents to estimate the proportion of burglaries, drug sales, and juvenile crime committed by African Americans found that white respondents overestimated the actual figures by 20 to 30 percent.[17]

These various perceptions and attitudes among whites then add up to greater support for punishment in racially charged ways. Criminologist Ted Chiricos and colleagues have conducted a series of projects designed to assess these linkages. One study examined a survey of public preferences for policies such as "making sentences more severe for all crimes," "executing more murderers," and "locking up more juvenile offenders." White respondents, who attributed greater crime rates for several offenses to blacks, were significantly more likely to support punitive policies. (The same was not true of African American or Latino respondents.)[18]

Similarly, in a 2012 study, Chiricos and colleagues found stronger support for harsh juvenile justice policies among those whites who were more likely to identify crimes as being associated with blacks. They concluded that "public support for punitive juvenile justice policies to some extent represents a desire to control other people's children."[19]

These racial perceptions and preferences are then likely to play out in regard to life sentences. As policy is developed—almost always in majority-white legislative bodies—punishments for crimes either actually or perceived to be committed by blacks in high proportion are likely to be influenced by racial perceptions. In the courtroom, as prosecutors make decisions about charging, as juries make decisions about guilt, and as judges make decisions about sentencing, racial perceptions are likely to push decision-making toward harshness.

Consider, for example, federal sentencing policy of recent decades in regard to drug sentencing. A wealth of research has documented that, despite the fact that use of illegal substances is roughly similar across racial/ethnic groups, law enforcement practices have both focused disproportionately on low-income communities of color and meted out harsher penalties for drug crimes associated with African Americans.[20] We have seen this most prominently in the crack cocaine era of the late 1980s and early 1990s, but similar dynamics have been emblematic of "drug wars" over many decades.

These racial assumptions then help us to understand in part why more than five hundred individuals, many of them people of color, who had been sentenced to life without parole for a third drug offense, received executive clemency during the Obama administration. These individuals were drug sellers and in many cases had several convictions, often for large quantities of drugs. Nonetheless, they had been sentenced more harshly than many individuals convicted of homicide, robbery, and other serious offenses.

Assessing the reasonableness of a life sentence requires a much broader examination than just looking at the crime of conviction. At each stage of the court process, the overlay of race and social class disadvantage increases the prospects that defendants of color will be most likely to receive the harshest punishments.

Even once sentenced to prison, lifers with the possibility of parole release will have a diminished likelihood of success if they come from families and communities with limited resources. The fact that parole board members seek candidates who have guaranteed housing and employment lined up prior to release severely reduces the odds that many poor lifers of color will be successful in gaining release.

The burgeoning reentry movement of recent decades offers hope that such disparities in decision-making can be alleviated. But to date, the scale of resources devoted to reforming such policies and implementing reentry programs is far too limited to produce a substantial impact on the group of individuals serving life sentences.

The Meaning of Life for Criminal Justice Reform

While the policy, financial, and moral issues surrounding mass incarceration have achieved increasing prominence in public discourse over the past decades, issues regarding long-term prisoners and those convicted of serious offenses have engendered little public discussion. The dramatic increase in the use of life sentences raises humanitarian concerns and is a major impediment to decarceration goals. Life imprisonment also has a direct influence on the overall punishment structure and poses challenges for the criminal justice reform movement.

Life Imprisonment Exacerbates the Severity of All Punishment

Along with the death penalty the extensive use of life imprisonment is in many ways an outgrowth of the American commitment to punishment rather than rehabilitation and reintegration. In turn, through the structure of the sentencing system, life sentences influence the scale of punishment and the development of mass incarceration.

Sentencing systems, whether determinate, indeterminate, or a mix of the two, are generally proportional in structure. The American Law Institute, a well-regarded, nonpartisan body of legal scholars, refers to the sentence for the most serious combination of offenses and individual circumstances as the "anchor point" for the sentencing structure. In a graduated system of punishment, the scale of severity will be proportional to the most severe penalty at the top of the scale. So murder is punished more harshly than robbery, which in turn is punished more harshly than burglary, and so on.

Virtually all industrialized nations other than the United States have repealed capital punishment and impose life imprisonment only sparingly. They therefore have a lower anchor point for punishment at the top of the scale, which serves as a moderating influence across all offenses. The contrast to sentencing policies in the United States can be seen most dramatically in the sentencing structure in Norway, a nation with a rate of incarceration of 74 per 100,000 (versus the United States' 666 per 100,000).[1] Following the tragic massacre of seventy-seven people (including sixty-nine individuals on the island of Utøya, most of whom were children) by Anders Behring Breivik in 2011, Breivik was sentenced to the maximum penalty for that crime, twenty-one years of imprisonment.[2] This penalty can be extended for five years at a time if it is determined that the individual still poses a threat to public safety.

To place some perspective on this, Weldon Angelos, a twenty-four-year-old music producer in the state of Utah, was convicted of three separate sales of marijuana of about three hundred dollars each to an undercover officer in 2002. On each of these occasions he was in possession of a weapon, which he neither used nor threatened to use. Because of the mandatory sentences that apply to many federal drug and gun crimes, the judge was required to sentence Angelos to fifty-five years in prison. Earlier on the day of sentencing, in the same courtroom, the judge in the Angelos case sentenced a man convicted of second-degree murder to twenty-two years for striking an elderly woman on the head with a log. At the time of sentencing, Judge Paul Cassell, a self-described conservative Republican, stated:

The court believes that to sentence Mr. Angelos to prison for the rest of his life is unjust, cruel, and even irrational. . . . It is also far in excess of the sentence imposed for such serious crimes as aircraft hijacking, second-degree murder, espionage, kidnapping, aggravated assault, and rape. . . . To correct what appears to be an unjust sentence, the court also calls on the President to commute Mr. Angelos's sentence to something that is more in accord with a just and rational punishment.[3]

Angelos did not receive a commutation but was freed on May 31, 2016, after a federal court granted him a reduced sentence.

The death penalty and life imprisonment at the top of the sentencing scale in the United States exert substantial upward pressure on sentencing severity throughout the sentencing structure, affecting penalties for car theft, larceny, assault, and other lesser offenses, as well as for more serious crimes. Thus, a mid-level drug seller in the United States can be punished far more harshly than a mass murderer in Norway.

While comparative research on sentencing severity is relatively limited, a 1990s review of sentencing severity among nations found that the United States is distinct in its tendency to require long sentences for offenses that do not involve serious violence.[4] Despite comparable rates of property crime and less serious violent offenses, the United States incarcerates at a higher rate and for longer periods than developed nations including England, Sweden, and Australia. Sentences in the United States are also much longer for drug offenses.[5]

The role of sentencing in contributing to mass incarceration has been documented by the National Research Council: the 222 percent growth in the rate of state imprisonment between 1980 and 2010 was *entirely* explained by changes in sentencing policy. Half of this effect was produced by an increased likelihood of incarceration per arrest and half by increases in time served in prison.[6]

Limitations of the Current Justice Reform Strategy

Since the late 1990s, a number of developments have raised the prospects for criminal justice reform for the first time in a generation. For a start, following a surge of violence, related in large part to the crack cocaine drug markets of the late 1980s that had contributed to a rise in homicide rates from 7.9 per 100,000 in 1984 to 9.8 per 100,000 in 1991, crime rates began declining in the early 1990s.[7]

The reasons for the crime decline are complex and not fully understood. But it appears that key factors included an improved economy in the 1990s, a decline of crack markets and their associated violence, changed policing strategies in some cities, the spread of anti-violence organizations, and more community engagement to dissuade young people from congregating at potentially troublesome locations. While large-scale incarceration is still claimed by some to have been a key factor in reducing crime, the National Research Council concluded that "the magnitude of the crime reduction [as a result of increased incarceration rates] remains highly uncertain and the evidence suggests it was unlikely to have been large."[8] As crime declined, the utility of the "crime issue" as a campaign platform for political leaders at all levels of government diminished as well. With public safety becoming less of a concern than other day-to-day issues, the number of campaigns focused on "getting tough" declined.

Movements both to challenge mass incarceration and to propose promising alternatives gained traction during this period. Most prominent was the growing opposition to the collection of policies comprising the War on Drugs, a major contributor to the growth of incarceration in the period of the 1980s and 1990s. From a variety of perspectives, drug policy came to be viewed as ineffective in controlling the supply, price, or use of illegal drugs.[9] In addition, concern grew about the fiscal costs of mass incarceration, the distortion of law enforcement priorities, and the broad racial disparities in the implementation of the drug war.

In the late 1990s, leaders at the Department of Justice advanced the concept of "reentry," a set of programs and policies designed to improve prospects for success for individuals returning home from prison.[10] Similar in many respects to the longstanding but by then politically discredited concept of rehabilitation, reentry captured the imagination of a broad range of practitioners as well as leaders across the political spectrum.[11] Concurrently, initiatives designed to incorporate a greater array of treatment services and diversion from incarceration at sentencing gained traction, including, for example, "specialty courts," focused on issues related to substance abuse and mental health. And as state governments began to experience tight fiscal constraints, political leaders recognized that the rising cost of corrections was impinging on vital state services.[12]

The result was a shift in the political climate on issues of crime and punishment to the point where calls for a substantial reduction in incarceration became increasingly frequent across the political spectrum. Leading conservatives such as Newt Gingrich and Grover Norquist advocated for a substantial reduction in incarceration, and governors of both major political parties embraced reform strategies in a number of states.

This changing political environment, along with the reduced crime effect on prison admissions, has substantially reduced the rate of *growth* in the prison system since 2000. By 2015, a handful of states had even experienced prison population declines in the range of 15 to 30 percent for various time frames.[13] Nevertheless, the number of people incarcerated today exceeds two million individuals, and the overall picture is generally one of only modest decline. It is increasingly clear that achieving a substantial reduction in the number of imprisoned people will require a far more aggressive and deeper strategy.

Many advocates and policymakers have called for change in

drug law enforcement and sentencing in particular. While such steps would produce a more rational allocation of public safety resources, their impact on the rate of incarceration would be more modest than assumed by many, since the contribution of drug offenses to mass incarceration has declined in recent years.[14] This is due in part to a moderate reduction in drug arrests (whether because of reduced use and selling of drugs or discretionary decisions to scale back the volume of arrests by law enforcement), modification of harsh sentencing polices such as New York's "Rockefeller Drug Laws," and the expansion of drug courts and other programs designed to divert individuals with substance abuse problems into treatment rather than incarceration.[15]

A further limitation to achieving the scale of reform necessary derives from the fact that prison sentences for drug offenses are typically considerably shorter than for violent offenses. Though we document incidences of life sentences for drug offenses in various jurisdictions and have highlighted some of the most egregiously disproportionate cases, less than 3 percent of life sentences (5,300) are being served by those whose most serious offense was a drug crime. Thus in order to address mass incarceration meaningfully, we will need to reduce the time served in prison even for those convicted of violent crimes.

As reforms develop around reducing incarceration for drug offenses, a greater proportion of the people who remain incarcerated will be serving life sentences. As noted previously, a record one in seven imprisoned people is currently serving a life sentence.[16] In thirty-five states, at least one of every ten people in prison has already been incarcerated for a decade or more.[17]

The increasing use of life sentences poses additional obstacles to a decarceration strategy. Life without parole sentences are increasing as a proportion of life-sentenced prisoners (not including virtual life), rising from 27 percent in 2003 to 33 percent in

2016. The number of people serving these sentences has grown at nearly four times the rate of life with parole sentences during this period.[18] Since those with no prospect of parole will never leave prison (except under exceptional circumstances) their numbers are increasingly significant.

Even among individuals sentenced to life *with* the possibility of parole, release from prison has become increasingly unlikely, or at the very least, longer in coming. In decades past many state sentencing systems allowed for parole consideration of lifers after fifteen or twenty years in prison. While those statutes are largely still in place, discretionary decisions by governors and parole board officials in states such as Michigan and Louisiana have now imposed a "life means life" interpretation of the sentence.[19] As the Georgia State Board of Pardons and Parole noted in 1998, "There's a popular misconception that life in prison doesn't mean all of one's natural life. In just the last year there are 21 Georgia lifers who are no longer around to tell you differently."[20]

In addition to the impact on prison populations, decisions to deny opportunities for parole to prisoners whose original sentences implied they would have such opportunities raise profound questions about redemption, justice, and fairness. At the time these individuals were sentenced to prison, their sentencing judges were clearly aware of the prevailing statutes in their respective states and were therefore comfortable imposing a sentence that would allow for parole release after a reasonable period if parole officials viewed the risk and behavioral issues favorably.

Political initiatives of recent decades have expanded the breadth of life sentences as well. Following the high-profile adoption of the three-strikes law in California in 1994 about half the states enacted a variation on this policy, typically calling for a life sentence for a third conviction of a violent offense.[21]

Harsh mandatory penalties adopted by Congress in the 1980s

as an outgrowth of the country's notorious War on Drugs have also extended the net of offenders subject to life without parole terms. A 2013 study identified 3,278 individuals serving such terms for nonviolent offenses in the federal system and nine states.[22]

The Impact of the Justice Reform Movement on Life Sentences

The large-scale use of life imprisonment in the United States is clearly an outgrowth of the punitive developments that have produced mass incarceration, and it is reasonable to think that the movement to end mass incarceration might have a positive effect on life sentences. Unfortunately, that has not been the case. Indeed, the mass incarceration reform movement itself increasingly poses challenges to policy changes for life sentences. This emerges both indirectly from campaigns and policy initiatives designed to reduce the scale of incarceration by addressing low-level offenses, and, in a more direct way, from the movement to abolish the death penalty.

A key objective of the criminal justice reform movement in recent years has been to reduce prison admissions and/or length of sentences for persons convicted of lower-level offenses, particularly drug crimes. Incarcerating such individuals has not been shown to produce any significant deterrent or incapacitating effects. It fails to address the underlying factors contributing to these persons' engagement in crime, and it can be seen as criminogenic (exposing individuals convicted of nonviolent offenses to those with a history of violence). It is also very costly to taxpayers. Yet this focus on low-level offenses excludes other categories of prisoners, including those serving life sentences, from reform efforts.

Another element of the reform movement has been to prioritize admitting persons charged with low-level offenses to diversion programs in order to build up a track record of success, with the idea of expanding to more serious cases later on. (In recent decades growing attention has been paid to restorative justice as a means of establishing more constructive consequences for criminal behavior; to date most of these initiatives have focused on lower-level offenses that would not otherwise result in lengthy prison terms.) Unfortunately, expansion of these programs to other offenses is rarely the case. Instead, policies, practices, and cultural assumptions become focused on the initial nonviolent program client profile, and the idea of expanding diversion to more serious cases becomes increasingly dim.[23]

In some cases reformers have actively campaigned to demonize those convicted of more serious offenses as unworthy of consideration for sentencing reform. The goal of the 2012 campaign in California to scale back that state's three-strikes law through Proposition 36, for example, was to require that all three strikes necessary to impose a sentence of twenty-five years to life be serious or violent offenses, rather than to make the case against all such draconian sentences.[24] The strategy employed by the reform campaign centered on making a sharp distinction between those convicted of violent offenses and all others. In launching the campaign, a spokesperson stated that "what the voters wanted in the first place was to make sure the *truly most violent monsters* are locked up forever" (emphasis added).[25] Thus, in trying to reduce the use of life imprisonment for some, the campaign unnecessarily demonized thousands of others.

The ballot campaign was in fact successful, gaining 69 percent public support for the reform, which in just the first two years after passage resulted in 1,613 people being released from custody.[26] But there may be long-term negative consequences both for lifers and for the prison population generally. By lending support to public perception that makes a sharp distinction between "deserving" individuals and the "truly most violent monsters," the advocates of limited reform are essentially calling for cutting off any exploration of what a broader conception of justice might look like—one that offers a more humane "anchor point" even for those who have committed serious offenses.

What might such an exploration look like? One could begin with assessing the backgrounds of the individuals who have ended up serving life sentences. What was their home and community life like? To what extent did they experience abuse, witness violence in the home or community, experience educational failure, and/or suffer from mental or physical disabilities? None of these issues would excuse or condone the harm they caused to others, but they would help us to understand something about the factors contributing to acts of violence and how we might prevent and respond to them.

Findings on the topic of childhood experiences from our national survey of individuals serving juvenile life without parole are quite disturbing, but illuminate the complicated life experiences before these crimes, as well as methods of coping with life imprisonment at a young age.[27] Respondents experienced high levels of violence as children, with 79 percent witnessing violence in their homes, and more than half witnessing weekly violence in their neighborhoods.[28] They also suffered high rates of sexual abuse: 21 percent of all juvenile lifers, and 77 percent of girls, reported such abuse. Many had experienced significant social and economic disadvantage: one-third had been raised in public housing, and 18 percent had not been living with a close adult relative at the time of their incarceration.[29]

These sobering patterns are now a vital part of discussions on extreme sentencing for youth, as articulated by Justice Kagan in the juvenile life without parole case *Miller v. Alabama*. As previously discussed, the sentencing of youth in adult court is now required to take into account the young age of the defendant and his or her limited culpability as a result.

But the successful litigation in the U.S. Supreme Court regarding juveniles serving life without parole sentences poses challenges for adults facing life sentences. Much of the argument for these campaigns focused, appropriately, on the fact that "children are different." Emerging research on brain development has strengthened the understanding that youth are not fully formed in their capacity to appreciate the consequences of their actions or to control impulsivity until their mid-twenties. In its rulings on the cases, the Court, invoking its opposition to death sentences for juveniles from *Roper v. Simmons*, noted, "Juveniles are more capable of change than are adults, and their actions are less likely to be evidence of 'irretrievably depraved character' than are the actions of adults. It remains true that '[f]rom a moral standpoint it would be misguided to equate the failings of a minor with those of an adult, for a greater possibility exists that a minor's character deficiencies will be reformed.'"[30]

But if "children are different," what does this say about adults, who are presumably more mature, less impulsive, and more culpable for their actions? Rather than casting adults as "deserving" of their punishments, we should instead extend the framework of the argument for juveniles to consideration of adult behavior. What would an individualized approach to sentencing tell us about considerations for length of sentence for adults who have committed serious acts? Sentencing using this framework would involve a consideration of issues of substance abuse and mental health for a start, both of which are all too common among those in prison. Routine exposure to violence and familial incarceration would be other factors to consider. Individualized sentencing would also involve realistic considerations of public safety concerns, such as an assessment of the degree to which risk declines with age and the availability of resources to aid individuals in their transition back to the community.

We are keenly aware of the political challenges that the justice reform movement faces at all levels of government. Advocacy for justice reform has for far too long been considered too controversial for political leaders in both major parties. Media sensationalism, politically inspired distortions of crime issues, and public fear have been major driving forces opposing any type of reform. Concern for public safety should clearly be a goal for any community.

But too often those concerns are expressed with little evidence to support proposed changes at best, and with racist assumptions at worst. And many proposed reforms have the effect of throwing whole categories of prisoners under the proverbial bus, rather than advancing ideas of lower anchor points and reduced individualized sentences across the board in a quest for a fairer, more humane sentencing system. With crime rates having declined over two decades and increasing concern about the harmful consequences of mass incarceration, we are now in a moment of strong grassroots advocacy for reform, with bipartisan support in a number of state legislative bodies as well as the U.S. Congress, along with heightened media attention to this crisis. In order to take advantage of this evolving environment, we would be well served by a movement for sentencing reform that is practical in its examination of new policies while visionary in seeking justice and fairness.

Kelly Garrett and Justin Singleton

An intense feeling washed over Kelly Garrett when first she held the hand of the man she would come to love. They had just met through his mother, Kelly's longtime coworker, who often spoke to Kelly of her son. "Justin was sitting to my left and we blessed the lunch food and we all held hands," she told me during a conversation at a coffee shop across the street from a classroom building at the University of Louisiana at Lafayette, where the former television executive turned activist was waiting to speak to a criminal justice class. "And literally, I felt energy come from his hand to mine." Her first thought was, "This is him." Her second, immediately following, "No, it's not."

It is among the most normal and coveted of social interactions, meeting someone with whom she felt instant chemistry. Or, it would have been except for the location—the Main Prison visiting room at the Louisiana State Penitentiary (also known as Angola). "Here's this man serving a life sentence," she said, "and I immediately dismissed that first thought." Kelly had never been to a prison—she knew no one who was incarcerated—and while she was naïve about criminal justice she was not naïve about life.

Kelly is a thirty something, college-educated, biracial single mother who, for nearly a decade, managed a Lafayette-area television station's digital division. "My daughter and I were living an ideal life. It was like I couldn't ask for anything else, but deep down there was a void," she said. Kelly is also a spiritual woman with a deep personal faith. "I've always had a prayer, ever since I was little, to have a purpose."

At the pinnacle of her career, making six figures and engaged for the second time to the same man, she found the resolve to break it off six weeks before her wedding because she knew in her heart that it wasn't right. "That was one of the biggest decisions I've ever made," she said. "After making it, and being okay with it, I decided to scoot over and let God drive. Two months later I was invited to go to Angola."

After the prison lunch meeting, Kelly and Justin's mother went to hear him preach at the prison chapel. Justin, an African American prisoner in his thirties, is also a pastor. "It felt like he was preaching to me, what I was going through in my life at the time." It was all part of a yet-undefined transformation that found Kelly questioning the path and purpose of nearly everything in her life.

Surprised and enlightened by many things she saw on that random visit to prison, she was much more deliberate about what came next. The experience proved to be a seminal moment in Kelly's life, one that would lead to her commitment to bring real, sustained change to criminal justice in Louisiana.

Over the course of months Kelly and Justin Singleton developed a deepening friendship, then something more emotionally intimate. "Ever since then that was it," she said. "I was hesitant about getting involved, about allowing myself to become involved with him. It took prayer and personal confirmation to know that this is where I needed to be." More than two years since that first meeting, Kelly is now unambiguously convinced that she has found not only her partner but her purpose. The process, however, has not been without doubt.

Justin was twenty-two in March 2003 when he and a co-defendant were arrested and charged with first-degree murder in a robbery/murder in a rural South Louisiana parish. It was Mardi Gras. Justin and his childhood friend were heading to the cele-bration in nearby Lafayette. On the way, with Justin driving, they stopped at a small store and his friend went inside. Justin stayed in the car listening to music. His friend came out, got back in the car, and they continued their drive to Lafayette. A few miles down the road they were stopped by the police. Inside the store, the of-ficer told Justin, the owner had been robbed, shot, and killed. The owner's wife, in the back asleep, heard nothing, but a witness saw a man about five feet nine inches tall come out of the store and get into a car before it drove off. Justin, who is six foot three, stead-fastly asserts he had no knowledge of what happened inside the store, before or after the crime. In the end, both men received life without the possibility of parole.

For Kelly, who saw something in Justin she had not expected, a cognitive dissonance developed between the man she had come to know—a kind, decent, patient man who earned a bachelor's degree in Christian ministry through the prison's extension campus of the New Orleans Baptist Theological Seminary and who also serves as a reentry vocational mentor—and the criminal justice system's label of convicted murderer. It was a gap she felt compelled to close.

It wasn't long after they met that Kelly was laid off from her job. Financially stable with no pressure to find immediate employment, she suddenly had time to tap into what she calls her "nosy and in-quisitive" nature. She began meticulously reviewing reams of doc-uments she received from Justin, and doing so pushed her to learn more. She spent days at the courthouse going through the public records about the crime and trial, and in short order she became an expert on the case. The research erased her original doubts, but a few new ones were created, these about the process itself. Her growing understanding of Louisiana's criminal justice system as dysfunctional was the catalyst that transformed her approach from apathy to advocacy.

With her sense of purpose growing, Kelly discovered critical information about Justin's case. It quickly became clear that the prosecution strategy, with Justin being tried first, was to use two different theories of the case, pointing at both men, in their respective trials, as the trigger man. But her discoveries told a different story, and it led to the revelation that Justin's co-defendant had admitted to his parents and to Justin's lawyers his role as the sole perpetrator, a spontaneous and fateful decision that also ensnared his childhood friend and sent Justin to prison for life. The newly discovered information and confession are now the basis of an appeal that Justin hopes will lead to his freedom. "He told me that he had not been this close to his freedom in fifteen years. Had it not been for me losing my job, I would have never gone to the clerk's office to find out what I found, and have my doubt, bring it to Justin and resolve it, and then his co-defendant having this change of heart."

After learning what she did through Justin's case, Kelly was more convinced than ever that she needed to be a voice that was heard. "Nothing changes if we just sit back and let it happen. I am educated, articulate, and I felt that if I am going to stay in Louisiana I need to make a difference. I have definitely found my purpose."

Now, advocacy is second nature for Kelly, who has been making her mark on the criminal justice reform landscape in Louisiana, focusing on the state's high rate of incarceration. In 2017, the legislatively appointed Justice Reinvestment Task Force proposed a historic package of reform bills. In the mix was Kelly, becoming active in several organizations from the grassroots advocacy group CURE to a newly formed umbrella group, Louisianans for Prison Alternatives. She was instrumental in creating a bill to change the time calculations for individuals sentenced to life without parole to apply for clemency. The reform bill passed, but not without compromise. Also in the bill was a provision to allow reapplication from a denial from five years to three years, but there was pushback from the powerful District Attorneys Association. "The authors called me and said there would have to be a compromise for it to survive. I had to choose." She quickly understood how the politics of power served to create the dysfunctional system she now seeks to change. "You know, it's been a while since I've taken civics. I was amazed at the process. There is no logic to it. This is how laws get passed? It's crazy. I don't understand why both elements could not pass. It's all about power, about not giving in."

Kelly's family is accepting and supportive of her relationship with Justin and her advocacy work. That, too, started with doubt, though now that Kelly's mother has been fueled by her fire she also works as an advocate. "When they first found out I was see-ing someone in prison they were not pleased and were judgmental, something I did not expect from them, a biracial couple, consider-ing what they went through." Kelly confronted what she now sees as protectiveness and says, "I guess it had an effect."

Her coworkers are also supportive. She doesn't hide it, nor does she broadcast it. "The people around me see my passion and, be-lieve me, nobody's immune to what actually goes on in our criminal justice system." She is prepared for the worst, understands reality, and accepts that, despite what her "nosy curiosity" turned up to help Justin, the system is not designed to fix errors. "In Louisiana, what seems to be an easy decision could be just the opposite."

How did the woman with a seemingly ideal life change course to become a criminal justice advocate, one who was recently hon-ored by the Lafayette chapter of the League of Women Voters for her work? "I just wasn't happy. I didn't feel fulfilled. I didn't feel like I was helping anybody. This was my prayer, give me some-thing that is worthwhile, that means something, that when I die people will know that I cared. I don't want a legacy of just making money. I want a legacy of doing something that makes a difference. I wouldn't trade this path in for anything."

The Meaning of Life for Public Safety

For several decades prior to 1973, the state and federal prison population in the United States had remained at roughly the same level. No one would have predicted that the coming year would mark the beginnings of mass incarceration, an unprecedented four-decade expansion of the American carceral system that has vaulted the United States to the dubious distinction of the world's largest jailor. In fact, proposals to advance *decarceration* were the most prominent feature of discussions about criminal justice in the early 1970s. For example, in the highly regarded book *Struggle for Justice*, the Quaker-led American Friends Service Committee called for the length of prison sentences to be "vastly reduced" because "excessively long sentences damage the individual and have not proved effective as general deterrence."[1] This proposal to cut prison terms came at a moment when the national prison population stood at a level *less than one-seventh* of what it is today.

In 1973, a particularly far-reaching sentencing proposal was issued: capping prison terms in most cases at a maximum of five years, with no allowance for a mandatory minimum. The only exceptions were sentencing for murder and a small number of other circumstances, where up to a twenty-five-year term would be authorized if necessary for the protection of the public.[2] This recommendation was not issued by religious reformers or civil liberties organizations but rather by the National Advisory Commission on Criminal Justice Standards and Goals,[3] established by President

Richard Nixon in 1971. Nixon's commission was itself an out-growth of the President's Commission on Law Enforcement and Administration of Justice created by President Lyndon Johnson, which had produced a set of widely circulated recommendations for criminal justice reform. The subsequent Nixon commission had as its mandate the task of taking the earlier commission's general proposals for reform and creating specific and verifiable goals for improving the justice system and reducing crime.

The National Advisory Commission was chaired by Republican governor Russell W. Peterson of Delaware, with Peter Pitchess, sheriff of Los Angeles County, as vice chair. Its members included leading scholars and practitioners in the field, such as then Phil-adelphia district attorney and future U.S. senator Arlen Specter. Their recommendations for criminal justice policy and practice grew out of a multi-year study and engagement with justice system practitioners around the nation.

Following its review of sentencing policy, the Commission con-cluded that "it has generally been recognized that American prison terms are too long" and that "with the exception of a relatively few dangerous offenders, there is no evidence that long prison terms offer more protection to the public than short terms." Calling at-tention to the negative consequences of incarceration, such as the economic cost and isolation from the community, the group called for prison terms to be "drastically reduced."[4]

The five-volume report by the Commission also contained rec-ommendations for professional development for criminal justice practitioners, restructuring of various components of the criminal justice system, and improving information technology, many of which were adopted by state and local governments in the years to come. But in the area of sentencing policy, not only was the five-year proposal disregarded, but over time legislators of both parties at all levels of government came to support a previously unimag-inable scale of harsh sentencing policies that largely remain the hallmark of the justice system today, with little regard to impact on public safety.

Four decades since the Commission's report we now have even more conclusive evidence that long-term sentences are counterproductive for public safety goals. They impose excessive punishment that is far out of line with any reasonable consideration of their utility and as such stand as a major contributor to the unprecedented scale of the prison population in the United States, without reducing the crime they are ostensibly needed to address.

Life Sentences and Diminishing Returns for Public Safety

The more than two hundred thousand people currently serving life sentences in the nation's prisons have overwhelmingly been convicted of serious or violent crimes. This raises important questions about the public safety implications of considering lifers for parole or compassionate release.

But examining these questions through the lens of the traditional sentencing goals of incapacitation, deterrence, punishment, and rehabilitation both exposes the limitations of excessive punishment and suggests an approach to public safety that better reflects public values about the role and nature of punishment.

Incapacitation—"Aging Out" of Crime

Common sense suggests incarcerating people who have committed serious offenses should be an effective way to enhance public safety, since incarceration renders them unable to commit crimes in the community while confined. Though this observation is correct in some respects, it is also more complex than might first appear. Holding people behind bars for long-term sentences inevitably results in diminishing returns for public safety. This is largely due to the well-documented finding that individuals "age out" of crime.

Readers over the age of thirty or forty can confirm the validity of this insight from their own lives. In our teen years and early twenties, most of us committed various violations of the law: illegal drug use, trespassing, small acts of vandalism or theft, driving without a license, or simple assaults. Whether or not we were detected or punished in some manner for these actions, by middle age most of us became far less likely to engage in such behaviors.

For most types of offending, basic factors help to explain this life transition. Since young people generally have less money than adults and fewer opportunities to earn money legitimately, they are more likely to be tempted to engage in stealing or drug-selling as a means of picking up spending money. Crimes such as household burglary require greater agility or strength, attributes that decline with age.

As we age out of the teen years we become adults, not only chronologically, but by taking on adult roles and responsibilities in society. We enter the world of work, find life partners, and become parents and homeowners. These adult roles are ones we view with pride, and they enhance our self-worth. We come to appreciate the benefits they provide, and, conversely, the risk of socializing with friends who are plotting the next theft of a six-pack from the local convenience store becomes less appealing. For most adults, there is simply less time, motivation, and opportunity to get into trouble.

It is also the case, of course, that adults of any age do not always lead entirely crime-free lives. Millions of seemingly upstanding Americans routinely cheat on their taxes by falsifying deductions or receiving pay under the table. Illegal drug use and sales continue for many people across all incomes. Those in the upper income brackets commit crimes such as insider trading and embezzlement.

There is also a group of individuals frequently described as "chronic offenders." These tend to be people whose troubling life circumstances contributed to their delinquency from an early age. Too frequently, their family histories include parents who themselves were in and out of the criminal justice system and childhood communities decimated by job loss and declining social safety supports, often for reasons relating to substance abuse or untreated mental illness. There follows poor performance in school, repeated delinquent acts including shoplifting and alcohol and drug use from a young age, and referrals to the juvenile justice system.

But while these individuals take longer to "age out" of crime, they are nonetheless also much less of a public safety risk at the age of forty than they were at twenty. The challenge for the community at large is to develop more robust rehabilitation programming in prison and to create pathways to opportunity and reentry services for the transition back to the community in order to prevent individuals from relapsing into destructive behaviors. (A related challenge lies in dismantling the punitive nature of many school environments—particularly low-income schools—which have created and expanded the "school-to-prison pipeline.")

The general tendency to "age out" of the high-crime involved years has been documented across social classes and national borders. In a comprehensive review of studies in this area, criminologists Rolf Loeber and David Farrington conclude that involvement in crime rises sharply in the mid-teen years, but then declines from the early twenties on. These findings are the same whether measured by arrest data or self-report data.[5]

As seen below in arrest data for robbery by age from the Bureau of Justice Statistics for 2014 (the most recent data available) the peak age for robbery is nineteen, with the rate declining by more than half by the late twenties. Similarly, the peak age for murder is twenty, a rate that is more than halved by the early thirties and is less than one-quarter of its peak by the early forties; for aggravated assault the peak age is twenty-two, with the rate more than halved by the early forties. These trends hold up for offenses not subject to life imprisonment as well. For example, burglary rates peak at

Arrest Rates by Age for Robbery, 2014

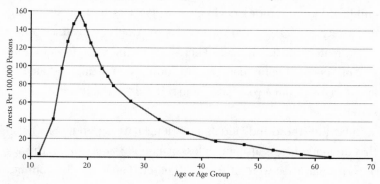

eighteen and are well under half that figure by the early thirties. In general, peak offending for violent crimes tends to be at a somewhat later age than for property crimes, and girls peak at an earlier age than boys.[6]

Loeber and Farrington note that while the age-crime curve is universal, young males growing up in disadvantaged communities of color with poor legitimate and meaningful job prospects have a greater prevalence of involvement in crime in the teen years and a longer period before those levels are substantially reduced. Those findings are in keeping with the understanding that taking on adult roles, such as stable employment, is a key factor in explaining desistance from crime. As criminologist Marieke Liem notes, it is the quality of these adult roles that makes a difference in desisting from crime.[7] It's not just the fact of having a job, but a question of a job that brings with it some sense of personal satisfaction and hope for the future. Many middle-class professionals can recall summer jobs working in a fast food franchise, but they regarded these jobs as a way to make spending money before going back to college in the fall. Similarly, marriage and romantic partnerships in themselves don't necessarily have a crime-reducing effect unless they are experienced as cohesive relationships that aid in personal growth and support. These insights help us to understand in part why some individuals remain active in crime longer than others. Criminologist Alex Piquero's research validates that criminal careers generally are "of a short duration (typically under 10 years)," even for the relatively small group of individuals who are frequent offenders. Here, too, he finds that "crime declines with age *even for active offenders*" (emphasis in original).[8] Brain development and maturity also relate to the age-crime curve.

This relatively new scientific finding has been acknowledged most notably in a series of rulings by the U.S. Supreme Court since 2005, first striking down the death penalty for juveniles and then scaling back the imposition of life sentences for individuals under the age of eighteen at the time of their offense. Drawing on brain research by Elizabeth Cauffman and Lawrence Steinberg, the Court concluded in the *Roper* decision abolishing the juvenile death penalty that in comparison to adults juveniles lack maturity and a sense of responsibility.[9] Writing for the majority, Justice Kennedy concluded that "juveniles are more vulnerable or susceptible to negative influences and outside pressures" and that "the character of a youth is not as well formed as an adult." While we somewhat arbitrarily set the age of adult maturity for drinking, smoking, joining the military, voting, and other behaviors at eighteen or twenty-one, in fact brain development is now more widely recognized as continuing until the mid-twenties.

Even among individuals whose prior record indicates significant public safety concerns, an understanding of the capacity for change and recognition of such change by the justice system is critical in establishing limits on excessive sentencing. This can be seen clearly in the spate of sentence commutations issued by President Obama in the last years of his second term in office.

Because the federal prison population had mushroomed, largely driven by the large-scale incarceration of people convicted of drug offenses, civil rights and civil liberties organizations had increasingly called for reform, along with legal groups, federal judges, and growing numbers of high-profile conservative leaders. Congress partially addressed the disparity in sentencing for crack cocaine offenses in 2010, but relief for other mandatory penalties was not successful. In response, President Obama used the executive clemency power to reduce the prison terms of 1,715 individuals serving these prison terms, nearly a third of whom were serving sentences of life without parole, typically for repeat drug convictions.[10]

A U.S. Sentencing Commission analysis of the prisoners who received these commutations shows a cross-section of individuals who would typically be left out of reform conversations about ways to reduce the prison population.[11] Nearly a quarter of the group receiving a commutation had a prior conviction for a violent offense, a third had a weapon involved as part of their current offense, 86 percent had a "significant criminal history," and 40 percent had a serious prison misconduct incident. Nevertheless, after a thorough review, the Office of the Pardon Attorney and the White House concluded that these individuals had changed substantially over their years of incarceration and presented a relatively low risk for public safety. In effect, they had "aged out" of crime.

Deterrence: Certainty versus Severity of Punishment

Policymakers frequently invoke the concept of deterrence and "sending a message" as the reason for proposing harsh sentencing policies. For example, in response to the March 2018 announcement by President Donald Trump that drug offenders should be sentenced to death as a means of addressing the opioid crisis, Attorney General Jeff Sessions stated, "We do not allow drug dealers to walk our streets, thinking they will get away with their crimes or that they will get a slap on the wrist. They need to know that we will not hesitate to pursue the maximum sentences allowed by law. And if appropriate, the death penalty." [12]

Similar sentiments can be heard in regard to the purported value of life imprisonment, and fears are raised that reducing the time served by lifers might harm public safety by reducing the deterrent effect of incarceration. While "sending a message" is compelling as a campaign slogan, it conflicts with a wide body of research evidence on deterrence.

Deterrence theory generally describes two types of effects: *individual* and *general*. Individual deterrence models suggest that the pain and suffering caused by a prison term will discourage those who have been through the experience from becoming engaged in crime again after they have been released. General deterrence theory posits that, because we all view the experience of going to prison as negative and see harsh prison sentences being meted out to those who commit infractions, we will be fearful of those consequences and will be less likely to commit crime.

While such effects may feel intuitively obvious at first, the general deterrent effect is actually nuanced. A wide body of research over time has concluded that the deterrent effect of the criminal justice system is primarily a function of the *certainty* of punishment, not its *severity*. That is, if we can increase prospects that a lawbreaker will be apprehended, some potential offenders will reconsider their plans. But since most people who commit crimes assume that they will likely not be apprehended for any given offense, they are not terribly focused on the scale of punishment. These assumptions hold true for crimes ranging from shoplifting to murder.

We all experience these dynamics in our everyday lives. Driving on a highway, most of us exceed the speed limit by some amount on a routine basis. Folk wisdom and experience tell us that driving 60 mph in a 55-mph zone most likely will not result in a speeding ticket, but driving faster than that would increase the odds of apprehension. Few of us know the cost of a speeding ticket on a given highway. It might be $50 or $150, but it's the prospect of apprehension that affects our behavior, not the severity of punishment.

Similarly, for criminal activity, consider the situation of a teenager with no money in his pocket thinking about snatching a Snickers bar from the local 7-Eleven store. He likely has no idea what the specific penalty for being caught is. He snatched one successfully last week, and he thinks he can probably get away with it again. But as he enters the store he notices that there's now a guard at the door, or that a security camera has just been installed. He knows that the odds of success have just changed and that he faces an increased risk of apprehension. He may decide to take a chance anyway, but the risk calculation is focused on the possibility of being caught, not what the potential penalty will be. Indeed, research has shown that most people who commit crime are not aware of the legal penalties they will face.[13]

The above examples explore how a rational person would respond to a shifting calculation of the odds of apprehension or punishment. But this hardly describes the general mental state of people considering committing a crime. Data from the Bureau of Justice Statistics show that about four in ten people in state prisons in 2009 reported that they were under the influence of drugs at the time they committed their offense.[14] These proportions are the same for those convicted of a violent offense, the crimes most likely to result in a life sentence. Since these people can hardly be considered rational actors weighing the consequences of committing a crime or even the likelihood of being caught, the deterrent effect of the certainty of punishment is limited as well. In addition, 14 percent of individuals incarcerated for a violent offense report that they committed their crime in order to obtain money to buy drugs (though there may be some overlap with those who were under the influence of drugs at the time of the offense).

Daniel Nagin, the preeminent American scholar on the issue of deterrence, has reviewed the research on the impact of deterrence on criminal activity. He concluded in a 2013 overview of scholarship that "the evidence in support of the deterrent effect of the certainty of punishment is far more consistent than for the severity of punishment,"[15] and that the effect of certainty is essentially a function of the certainty of apprehension.[16] In simple terms, consider the impact of increasing the mandatory prison term for a third-time drug crime from twenty years to twenty-five years. It is difficult to imagine that a person would blithely engage in such an offense if the penalty were *only* twenty years but would balk at doing so if it increased to twenty-five years.

While these findings represent sophisticated research during the era of mass incarceration, their genesis is centuries old. As far back as the eighteenth century, the Italian legal philosopher Cesare Beccaria in his treatise *On Crimes and Punishments* attacked the death penalty on the grounds that the state had no right to take a life but also because he saw no deterrent effect of the sanction.[17] For crime in general Beccaria concluded that both the certainty and the celerity (swiftness) of punishment produced a much stronger effect than the severity of punishment.

Recidivism of Long-Term and Life Prisoners

While the research finding that the general population ages out of crime is well established, one could reasonably ask if the same is true of those given life sentences. Theoretically, this group of individuals should represent the most serious and/or chronic offenders in the population (even though the massive expansion of the prison system over four decades has swept up a large number of people convicted of less serious crimes as well). But a substantial number of studies of those released from sentences of life imprisonment because of parole, clemency, an overturned conviction, or another reason, show relatively modest rates of recidivism.

An early study in Michigan examined parole release outcomes for 175 individuals serving life sentences during the period 1937 to 1961. None committed another homicide, and only four (less than 2 percent) were returned to prison for other offenses. A Canadian study of 119 persons whose original death sentences were

converted to life imprisonment, and who were subsequently released between 1920 and 1967, found that one was convicted of
another homicide. More recently a 2011 study tracked 860 people convicted of murder in California who had been paroled since
1995. Only 1 percent were recommitted to prison or jail for a new
felony, and none received a new life term for their offense.[18]

Data produced by the Bureau of Justice Statistics for a cohort of
individuals released from prison in 1994 shows considerably lower
rates of recidivism for lifers than for other releasees. Lifers were
less than one-third as likely to be rearrested within three years
of release, and four out of five lifers were not rearrested. Of those
who were rearrested, lifers were less likely than the total cohort to
be charged with a violent offense (18 percent versus 22 percent).[19]

A 2013 review of more than twenty studies of recidivism for persons convicted of homicide lends additional depth to this analysis
and supports the argument that long prison terms produce diminishing public safety returns. The studies, conducted in both the
United States and a half dozen European nations, variously examined rearrest, reconviction, or re-incarceration for various offenses.
The author of the review concludes:

> This literature review indicate[s] that the prevalence of spe-
> cific recidivism [a subsequent homicide] is very low. On the
> other hand, recidivism is high when measured in parole vi-
> olations and new drug charges. Recidivism as measured by
> committing violent offenses seems to fall between the two ex-
> tremes, ranging from 2 to 16 percent.[20]

While not all persons convicted of homicide are sentenced to life
imprisonment, generally those convicted of homicide in any nation
will be subject to the harshest penalties in their respective sentencing structure. Thus, this review suggests that, in contrast to
dire predictions from parole opponents, there is a "very low" risk

of subsequent homicide offenses, while the greatest impact is on parole violations and new drug convictions. Such findings lend additional credence to the phenomenon of diminishing public safety returns from long prison terms.

Excessive Incarceration of Less Culpable Individuals
A blanket policy of long-term incarceration for serious crimes fails to take into account the likelihood that various individuals will commit future crimes. Consider two individuals incarcerated for a homicide. The first is a "hit man" for organized crime who has been convicted of killing a rival mob member and is suspected of having been involved in other murders as well. The second is a battered woman engaged in a fight with her abuser who picks up a kitchen knife and kills her partner. We can debate whether the battered woman needs to be incarcerated as an expression of societal norms, and she may need counseling and support to avoid future abusive relationships, but her crime is situational and not part of an ongoing engagement in criminal activity. The threat to public safety for the "hit man" is likely to be much higher than the threat for the battered woman, yet each may receive the same punishment.

Cost of Life Imprisonment: Diversion of Resources
A final problem with life imprisonment as a public safety strategy is that it provides little protection but at a very high cost. The diminishing returns for public safety of housing an increasing number of life-sentenced prisoners are magnified by the expense of housing a growing elderly population in prison. Given that imprisonment takes a toll on one's physical health, many scholars consider fifty-five as the age at which incarcerated individuals can be considered elderly. In recent decades, there has been dramatic growth in the over-fifty-five portion of the prison population. From 1993 to 2013 the number of elderly prisoners grew by 400 percent, from

26,300 to 131,500, of whom more than 50,000 had already served ten years.[21]

Largely due to health care needs, the cost of housing an aging prisoner has been estimated to be at least double that of a younger prisoner. The population of people entering prison is generally less healthy than the population at large, due to high rates of substance abuse and limited access to health care. As individuals age in prison, they have a high likelihood of suffering from cardiac disease, high blood pressure, hepatitis C, and other diseases. As a result, some states have now established geriatric and hospice units (or even entire institutions) within their corrections systems.

Public safety funds are finite, and resources devoted to elderly health care are not available to invest in expanding access to prevention and treatment. The billions of dollars spent to house an aging and increasingly low-risk population is robbing resources from societal needs that are far more pressing. As we have seen, a cohort of fourteen- and fifteen-year-olds is continually entering the high-crime-rate years. This period will be relatively short-lived for most but will involve high rates of criminal involvement for a subset of this age cohort versus extremely low rates of criminal involvement for individuals aged fifty-five and older, including those who committed violent offenses earlier in their lives.

Reallocating funds spent on housing elderly prisoners to enhance prospects for good schooling, job opportunities, housing, and substance abuse treatment in under-resourced neighborhoods would be both more compassionate and more effective in stemming crime problems and the influx of young people into jails and prisons. Research evidence shows that investments in preschool education, parent-training programs such as the Nurse-Family Partnership,[22] and housing mobility through Moving to Opportunity[23] both improve outcomes for education and behavioral issues and reduce long-term contact with the criminal justice system.

Public safety does not benefit by simply imposing longer and harsher punishments. Instead, reallocation of resources to prevention supports individuals in escaping environmental factors that are associated with crime. In addition, enhancing the certainty of arrest for crimes when they do occur, rather than lengthening prison terms, will have a greater deterrent effect. Finally, sentencing practices that allow consideration of individual factors that precipitate a crime will result in more appropriate outcomes overall.

Enacting a Twenty-Year
Maximum Sentence

To lay the groundwork for a realistic challenge to mass incarceration and to provide a better approach to advancing public safety, sentences in American prisons should be capped at a maximum of twenty years, except in circumstances in which the individual still represents a clear threat to public safety. While this policy would mark a sharp course correction from the current U.S. sentencing system, it is not at all a radical goal when examined in the context of American historical policies, policies in other industrialized nations, or the findings of criminological research. While maintaining public safety, a policy shift in such a direction would reduce the dramatic harms that mass incarceration has brought to communities of color in particular, as well as address the human rights concerns that have become so stark in the past several decades.

Substantial evidence exists that a twenty-year maximum sentencing cap will produce better public safety outcomes than our current, record-breaking use of life imprisonment. This would lead to a better allocation of resources and would position the United States more in line with other industrialized nations in limiting the use of extreme sentences.

Such policies are supported by the experience of many other nations, as well as the research of esteemed legal scholars in the United States. The 2017 Model Penal Code of the American Law Institute concludes that "terms for single offenses in excess of 20 years are rarely justified on proportionality grounds, and are too long to serve most utilitarian purposes."[1] Instead, they propose a mid-course review for long sentences, recommending that a "judge or judicial panel revisit the sentence of any prisoner who has served 15 years or more in prison, and decide if, under present circumstances, the sentence originally imposed or a different sentence better serves the purposes of sentencing."[2] The "second look" would examine changed circumstances since sentencing, which might mean changed societal assessments of offense gravity; new technologies of risk assessment or treatment; or major changes in the individual, their family circumstances, the crime victims, or the community.

In order to adopt a twenty-year maximum prison term, a broad range of practical issues would need to be addressed, at both state and federal levels.

Need for Reentry Services

Replacing life imprisonment with a twenty-year maximum prison term is eminently defensible on grounds of public safety, cost-effectiveness, and human rights concerns. But this does not necessarily suggest that the impact of serving "only" twenty years in prison is negligible. Prison conditions in far too many institutions are degrading, are characterized by high levels of violence and abuse, and make the goal of maintaining family connections very challenging. Moreover, programming limitations ensure that few people emerge from long-term sentences with marketable job skills or educational attainment, in addition to the societal stigma that accompanies anyone with a prison record.

Thus, even more so than for other incarcerated people, long-term prisoners require comprehensive services and support in readjusting to the community if they are not to cycle back into the criminal justice system. Money saved on housing aging prisoners must be redeployed to ensure that those leaving prison after twenty years are equipped to re-enter society in a meaningful, self-sustaining way. As is true of all effective reentry programs, the transition period should begin well before the day of release and should include educational and rehabilitative services, extensive counseling on employment strategies and options, arranging for health care services, establishing stable housing, and reuniting with family members. Corrections officials should also have in place a plan for transitional services to be coordinated by a parole agency if appropriate, or human services networks in the home community. All of these services together can be provided for a fraction of the cost of incarcerating an aging prisoner for additional years.

One intriguing model for providing reentry services for lifers is the LifeLine Program that operated in Canada for two decades beginning in the 1990s.[3] The program employed released former lifers and long-term prisoners to serve as "In-Reach Workers," who in turn worked with volunteers within the federal prison system during their term in prison. The goal was to assist them in managing their prison term and to facilitate a structured and individualized release plan. At the height of the program's operation, nine non-governmental organizations across Canada were sponsoring LifeLine programs, which had reached 80 percent of the eligible population in the institutions. A 2010 study of the program by the Evaluation Branch of the Correctional Service of Canada concluded that the program aided lifers' ability to cope while incarcerated and facilitated greater program participation in the community for those who were released.[4] Despite such findings, in 2012 the Conservative government's "tough on crime" stance led to a complete cut in funding for the program.

Word of the LifeLine program had filtered into corrections circles within the United States, and in 2009 a Colorado corrections official, Tim Hand, went to Windsor, Canada, to observe its operation. Enthused by the potential of the program, Hand subsequently developed a similar model, the Long-Term Offender

Program, for Colorado. Working with parole-eligible lifers, the program targeted men with a strong prison record and reasonable prospects for parole release. A strong connection with locally based community corrections boards was established as a key step-down component of the transition from prison to the community, as well as engagement with CURE, a national prison reform group with state chapters.

Rod Thorpe was one of the successful graduates of the program. After a rough childhood in Alaska, Thorpe spent a year in a group home, began drinking heavily and using drugs, and described himself at the time as having "no regard for anyone, their feelings, nothing."[5] As part of a botched kidnapping, he ended up killing a sixteen-year-old boy and was sentenced to twenty years to life. Thorpe credits a sympathetic warden with having encouraged him to pursue his education, which became his passion. After more than two decades in prison, Thorpe was paroled with the support of the Long-Term Offender Program and became a mentor to men in a community halfway house. Thorpe notes that "We feel bad because of the pain and suffering we've inflicted upon others. Until you come to grips with that, the rest of you is a façade." In 2014 Thorpe earned his PhD while still focusing on helping young adults to earn their GED certificates.

Another program model addressing reentry needs following long-term incarceration has been developed by the Equal Justice Initiative in Alabama. Building on the initiative's work in successful legal challenges to the policy of juvenile life without parole, the Post-Release Preparation and Education Program was developed to meet the unique needs of individuals who were sentenced to lengthy prison terms and who entered prison between the ages of fourteen and sixteen. Program staff recognized that teenagers face significant vulnerabilities in the adult prison system and have fewer life management skills than adults. The program provides counseling in prison prior to release, followed by services including employment, mental health counseling, and vocational training upon release.[6]

To be successful, reentry services for lifers will need to be far more extensive than those provided in most reentry programs today. This will involve a greater allocation of public funds, but that is hardly an insurmountable challenge. The impact of a twenty-year cap on reduced prison populations and consequent cost savings will be quite substantial and could easily be redirected toward programming of this nature.

Public Safety Concerns and Identifying the "Exceptional" Cases

As previously documented, long prison sentences produce diminishing returns for public safety and come at great expense. While the behavior of any given individual is difficult to predict, in the aggregate, sentences of life imprisonment are excessive punishments for crime control purposes. Nonetheless, in any system of justice some number of people will present a threat to public safety even after twenty years of incarceration. One situation might be that of a person convicted of serial rapes who refuses to participate in treatment programming while in prison. In the absence of treatment, the public safety risk in such a case could be significant. Another case would be someone convicted of a terrorist offense who has not expressed remorse for his or her actions and believes they serve some greater good. Here, too, one can reasonably believe that the individual may be likely to reoffend if given the opportunity. Therefore, a structure is required to make the determination of who these individuals are and how they should be treated following the expiration of their prison term.

In order to make determinations of dangerousness following two decades of confinement, jurisdictions will need to establish some type of public safety review board. Such a structure would be similar in some respects to a parole board, but with significant distinctions. Most importantly, the members of the board would need to have expertise in offender assessment, suggesting the need for psychologists, social workers, and other therapeutic backgrounds. In contrast, many parole boards today consist of gubernatorial appointees, who in many cases represent campaign supporters of the executive branch or law enforcement personnel with no strong experience in assessing public safety risk.

Within the twenty-year structure of incarceration, prison staff could recommend to the review board in the final year of a prison term that an assessment be done for a particular individual.

Extended Confinement for the "Exceptional" Cases

For individuals who are deemed to be public safety risks after twenty years of confinement, a review board may recommend a period of civil confinement, similar to the process in Norway. The goal of such confinement would be to provide programmatic interventions designed to reduce the level of risk and ensure a safe transition back to the community, which should be the ultimate goal of *every* prison sentence. A jurisdiction might establish a policy of five years civil confinement, with an option to extend the confinement for additional terms if rehabilitative programming has not been successful. Alternatively, the period of civil confinement could be indefinite until such time as the risk level has been reduced.

Variations on this policy already exist in a number of U.S. states through civil confinement statutes that apply to persons convicted of a sex offense. The experience of these structures to date illustrates how a framework for addressing public safety risk can be developed, as well as the potential pitfalls in such a system.

In general, near the expiration of the criminal sentence, the state petitions to have the individual held in secure confinement within a treatment facility until such time as he is designated as a lower risk. The current generation of civil confinement laws for persons convicted of a sex offense traces its origins to a 1990 Washington State statute, the Community Protection Act, enacted in response to several high-profile crimes committed by people with prior sex offense convictions.[7] As of 2016, twenty states had such programs, holding a total of approximately 5,355 individuals under their provisions. By law and court rulings, these programs are required to be non-punitive in nature and are premised on the idea that therapeutic interventions can lead to eventual release back into the community.

In practice, release from civil confinement for those convicted of a sex offense is quite difficult for a number of reasons. Given the nature of the crime and of the individuals themselves, many of those confined have a history of being treatment-resistant. High-quality treatment is also quite expensive, typically costing at least one hundred thousand dollars annually per participant. Political considerations factor into release decisions, with a reluctance among many public officials to "take a chance" on releasing someone who might go on to commit a high-profile crime. As a result, a comprehensive review of civil confinement for persons convicted of a sex offense concludes that "release has been rare or nonexistent in many states, and even among those that have achieved modest success in moving clients through treatment, the pace of releases has nonetheless been exceeded by the growth in new commitment activity."[8]

While these findings are discouraging in regard to program preparation for release, a New York State model is premised on identifying high-risk individuals but is not solely focused on confinement. Through the Sex Offender Management and Treatment Act, passed in 1997, the state has established a multi-tiered process designed to accomplish the twin goals of rehabilitation and public safety.[9] The target group for consideration for program placement consists of people with a qualifying felony conviction (including most felony sex offenses and others that were sexually motivated) who have been diagnosed as having a mental abnormality that places them at high risk for a repeat sex offense.

Under the program, persons believed to fit the program criteria are referred for evaluation six months prior to a prison release date. Teams of licensed clinicians conduct intensive assessments of the individual, and if civil management is recommended the case is then referred to the Office of the Attorney General. Ultimately, a decision on dangerousness is made by a judge. Notably, this determination may include an order of either civil confinement or civil management, with the latter being community-based supervision and treatment under an order of Strict and Intensive Supervision and Treatment. A review of the New York screening and assessment process found that the state was able to identify high-risk individuals, leading to a reduction in rearrest rates for sex offenses. (The authors also note that these rearrests account for only about 5 percent of the total number of sexual offense arrests annually, thus calling attention to the need for broad-based prevention and treatment interventions involving the larger community.)

Other models of post-sentence confinement for the relative handful of persons who might be identified as dangerous after twenty years of confinement can be developed as well. The review of the experience with such confinement for persons convicted of a sex offense suggests that reasonable processes can be established to meet those goals, but that humane standards dictate that policymakers need to be careful to maintain a commitment to eventual release to the community.

It is also important to note that civil confinement, whether applied to people convicted of a sex offense or any other crime, is a form of preventive detention. As such, it represents inherent challenges regarding the power of the state to infringe on individual liberty. For example, even a group of individuals identified as "high risk" of reoffending will include a substantial number of "false positives"— people kept in detention who would in fact not have reoffended. What level of prediction error are we willing to live with in order to prevent crimes from a certain number of other people in the high-risk category?

We will need to enact a set of standards in order to reduce any unwarranted extension of civil confinement, and the burden of proof of dangerousness after twenty years of incarceration should be placed on the state. If after five years of civil commitment an additional period of confinement is to be considered, a similar process should be in place at that point as well. Jurisdictions should also develop standards that limit the types of offenses and/or individual behavioral issues that may be considered for civil confinement.

These issues are not unique to the area of civil confinement, and in fact are raised every day in the criminal justice system. Many jurisdictions, for example, incorporate a risk assessment of dangerousness into their pretrial release instruments used to make recommendations for release or detention prior to trial. Parole boards also conduct such assessments, both to aid in determining whether prisoners have engaged in prison programming designed to address their risk level needs and to establish conditions of supervision upon release to the community.

Thus, practitioners in the justice system make decisions on a regular basis regarding the public safety consequences of pretrial release, sentencing, and community supervision. But these decisions are made in the context of other goals of the system, which may include punishment, rehabilitation, and deterrence. Under civil confinement, by contrast, the premise of isolating the individual is that of preventive detention. We should be clear about the goals of such a process and cognizant of the risk of over-predicting and ensure that any period of confinement be focused on enhancing opportunities for the individual to be released back to the community at the earliest reasonable moment.

Retroactivity

Replacing life and long-term sentences with a twenty-year maximum raises a question of whether such shifts should be made retroactive and be applied to those who are currently serving such prison terms. Retroactive application of sentencing policies is not necessarily assumed in legislative reforms, and indeed has been the subject of significant legal controversy.

Most relevant to life imprisonment issues was the U.S. Supreme Court decision in 2016 where the Court was asked to make retroactive its prior decision in the case of *Miller v. Alabama* to bar the imposition of mandatory life without parole on juveniles. In *Montgomery v. Louisiana* the Court held that new rules of criminal procedure must be retroactive when there are new watershed procedural rules and substantive rules of constitutional law, and that the facts of the case met this requirement.[10]

The *Montgomery* decision affected an estimated 2,000 of the 2,500 such persons serving mandatory juvenile life without parole around the nation at the time. While the pace of resentencing these individuals and of states amending their sentencing statutes has been far too slow, nonetheless the process is in place. People sentenced under these policies are beginning to have their sentences altered, and some have been released to the community.

Aside from legal considerations, legislative bodies are free to establish new sentencing standards that are explicitly made retroactive. In the case of the twenty-year maximum sentence proposal, there is no moral justification for not extending this to persons already imprisoned under decades-long terms. If we as a society come to recognize that such sentences are excessive and unwise, why would that same rationale not apply to those convicted prior to the law change?

Some would argue that retroactivity should not apply due to the sheer scale of resentencing that would be required around the nation: with 206,000 people serving some type of life sentence, and additional others sentenced to between twenty and fifty years, a substantial bloc of people would be affected. But a burden on the justice system should not override considerations of justice. If individuals are incapacitated under conditions that are unjust or unconstitutional, that finding should override any short-term inconvenience to the system. Consider, for example, the U.S. Supreme Court's 2011 decision in the case of *Brown v. Plata*, in which the Court found that health conditions in the overcrowded California prison system were unconstitutional.[11] The Court ordered the state to address its severe overcrowding problem, which it accomplished through reducing the institutional population by 46,000 individuals over several years through its policy of "Realignment." That initiative restructured sentencing for nonviolent offenses so that most people convicted of them would be supervised at the local level, either in jail or on probation, rather than continuing to be housed in state prisons. No serious harms to public safety occurred as a result of this shift.

Not everyone subject to retroactive application of the law would need to be resentenced immediately. Some of the people serving life and long-term prison sentences were convicted fifty years ago, while others were convicted last week. State and federal officials could prioritize cases for resentencing starting with the longest-serving individuals. In most states it would be assumed that a life, or lengthy, sentence would be reduced to twenty years, but provisions might be made for individuals to argue for a lesser term based on individual circumstances.

States that maintain a system of sentencing guidelines can find an example of large-scale resentencing in a retroactive decision by the U.S. Sentencing Commission. Following on a multi-year review of sentencing policies for drug offenses, the commission reduced the severity levels for these offenses in its guidelines matrix in 2014.[12] About 48,000 individuals serving federal prison terms were affected by the shift, which granted potential recipients an average two-year reduction in sentence, if approved by a federal judge. Prosecutors and defense attorneys in each federal district worked together to process the cases. In the majority of cases no public safety concern was expressed to implementing the guideline change, a recommendation that was passed along to the sentencing judge. In cases without a consensus, the judge held an open hearing before making a determination of sentence. Ultimately, about two-thirds of the relevant cases were granted the sentence reduction.

A recent example of policy change in California illustrates this as well. In 2012, California voters approved an amendment to the state's three-strikes law, under which thousands of individuals had been sentenced to a prison term of twenty-five to life, even for such minor offenses as stealing golf clubs from a sporting goods store, a case that was upheld by the U.S. Supreme Court. The amendment established that all three strikes in such cases needed to be for a serious or violent crime and made this change retroactive. As a result, about 2,848 people became eligible for retroactive resentencing and are gradually being released from prison.[13]

Recalibrating Sentence Lengths for All Offenses

Life and decades-long sentences have been demonstrated to be a poor use of public resources, particularly since they produce diminishing returns for public safety as individuals age out of the crime-prone years. In addition, along with the death penalty they serve as an anchor point against which sentences for other offenses are established. Since sentencing structures of all types are generally proportional—more serious crimes result in longer prison terms—maintaining such a high anchor point produces longer sentence lengths for all offenses, regardless of their severity.

As we have seen, sentences for less severe crimes are considerably longer in the United States than in other industrialized nations, with no evidence that these dynamics produce better public safety outcomes. Indeed, their fiscal cost and lengthier separation of the individual from family and community contribute to a diversion of resources from rehabilitative programming and greater challenges for reentry. For a host of reasons, sentencing policy would be more appropriately calibrated if a twenty-year maximum prison term were to result in less punitive sentences across the board.

Achieving such an outcome would certainly be a challenging undertaking. Policymakers and practitioners in any large institution are generally slow to change decades-long patterns of behavior and decision-making. Further, many political leaders would contend that such an undertaking would be disruptive to court systems and would require a major investment of legislative resources.

Such arguments are not entirely without merit, but if policymakers come to accept the rationale for the twenty-year maximum prison term, they would then be wise to consider how to implement incremental shifts toward broader sentencing reform. In states with structured sentencing guidelines systems, for example, commissioners could initiate a process of annual guidelines amendments to shift sentencing standards gradually to a proportional structure more in line with the new upper limit.

Policymakers could also consider ways to shift practitioner decision-making over time. In part this would involve training and education for judges, prosecutors, and defense attorneys regarding the resource and public safety issues affected by varying levels of sentencing severity. Judges would be key actors in such a transition, since their buy-in over time would likely affect plea negotiations between the prosecution and defense in terms of their understanding of revised sentencing ranges.

Critics of a sentencing recalibration process will no doubt raise issues of workloads and resources involved to undertake such a process, and it is clear that these effects are not trivial. But these concerns need to be weighed against issues of inefficiency and injustice that currently characterize American sentencing policies. Failing to undertake such a process could only suggest that resource issues trump the pursuit of justice. Hopefully, policymakers will choose justice.

Reinvesting Prison Savings to Reduce Crime

A full recalibration of the American sentencing structure premised on a twenty-year maximum prison term would produce a dramatically lowered scale of incarceration. The cost of incarceration in state and federal prisons is estimated to be about $60 billion annually. If the number of people incarcerated were reduced substantially, investing even a portion of the financial savings in public safety initiatives would likely produce better outcomes and gain public support.

One model for investment is through the concept of justice reinvestment. Originally conceived with criminal justice advocates convened by the Open Society Institute, justice reinvestment envisions public safety as a function of a range of institutions and decisions in society, of which the criminal justice system is but one.[14] With the advent of mass incarceration, resources devoted to the justice system have been allocated at the expense of investments in prevention and treatment that would be far more effective in addressing crime.

To date the concept of justice reinvestment has played out most prominently through the Justice Reinvestment Initiative, a strategy led by the Pew Trusts, Council of State Governments, and other partners.[15] The initiative has primarily focused on shifting resources within the criminal justice system. For example, in a number of states cost savings from reductions in prison populations have been reallocated to providing enhanced services and resources for persons under community supervision, with a goal of reducing returns to prison. The groups have worked in both red and blue states and, while substantial reductions in prison populations have been difficult to achieve, they have helped to shift the conversation about the range of choices available to policymakers.

Using the justice reinvestment framework to shift resources outside of the justice system is more challenging. State and local budgeting processes normally allocate resources by type of public function, such as a Corrections Committee or an Education Committee within a state legislature. For both political and logistical reasons, it is much simpler to reallocate funds within a given area of public policy than across such lines.

Nevertheless, with a political commitment to enable such reallocations, such a transfer should not be unduly challenging. One current example of such a process is the Proposition 47 ballot proposal enacted by California voters in 2014.[16] By reducing the number of people in state prison for drug and property offenses, including through retroactive changes, substantial savings will be realized in reduced costs of incarceration. As of 2017, the California Department of Corrections was projecting savings of $103 million over a three-year period. The structure of the initiative requires that a substantial portion of these savings be directed to community-based services, including school dropout prevention, victim services, and mental health and substance abuse treatment.

The Tradeoff Between the Death Penalty and Life Without Parole

A major challenge in considering how to reduce sentence length is brought about by the troubled issue of the death penalty. As virtually the only industrialized nation that upholds capital punishment,[17] the United States maintains a death row population of nearly three thousand people. Over the past decade, however, support for the death penalty has declined significantly. This shift in the political climate, along with high-profile cases of innocent persons sentenced to death and then freed from prison after serving twenty years or more, has resulted in declining executions overall. From a recent high of ninety-eight in 1999, the figure steadily declined to twenty-three by 2017.[18]

But at least part of the decline in the use of the death penalty rests on the argument that another, equally effective option is available to judges: life sentences. Legal scholars Carol Steiker and Jordan Steiker observe that the "arguments, policies, and law relating to the death penalty have had a complicated, multidirectional spillover [effect] in the context of incarceration, and *vice versa*."[19] Indeed, Alabama, Illinois, and Louisiana all enacted life without parole statutes during the national moratorium on the death penalty between 1972 and 1976. The use of life sentences as an alternative to the death penalty is seen clearly through the annual data from a number of states. In Indiana, Mississippi, Ohio, South Carolina, and Texas, for example, declines in the death row population coincide with sharp rises in the life without parole population.

In states that have abolished the death penalty in recent years—seven in the past decade[20]—this has generally resulted in persons on death row being resentenced to life without parole as well as this becoming the standard sentence for crimes that previously would have resulted in a death sentence. But in practice this shift has also expanded the pool of defendants pulled into such sentences, which in effect are "death in prison" sentences.

As abolitionist campaigns have attacked the death penalty in state legislatures, they have done so on issues of morality, appeals to concerns about fiscal costs, and arguments about public safety. Typically, this has included a call for the replacement of the death penalty with life without parole sentences, both for those currently serving capital sentences and for future individuals who would otherwise have been sentenced to death. For attorneys litigating death penalty cases, a proposal for a life without parole sentence is often a critical tool used in jury trials and plea negotiations to avoid a death sentence. Advocating for life without parole as an alternative to the death penalty is perfectly understandable. The death penalty has been a fact of life in most states for many decades, and campaigning for its abolition is a major undertaking. Given that people on death row have been convicted of capital murder, it is not surprising that both the public and lawmakers would be focused on public safety concerns. The reform strategy of promoting life without parole as an alternative seeks to remove any doubt that the incarcerated person will ever be freed to kill again.

A key concern regarding this strategy, however, is that by advocating for life without parole, death penalty abolitionists may be contributing to an enhanced use of such sentences well beyond the numbers that would be generated if it were *only* an "alternative" to the death penalty. In New Jersey, for example, the repeal of the death penalty was accompanied by a statutory change that, according to a member of the state's study committee, mandated "imposition of life without the possibility of parole in countless cases in which the death penalty would never otherwise be imposed."[21] In contrast to the structure of the death penalty, which requires weighing aggravating and mitigating factors, a mandatory penalty of life without parole not only replaces death sentences but often also replaces sentences that would have allowed for the possibility of parole. This trend is supported by the rise in offenses that can trigger a life without parole sentence in the modern death penalty era that go far beyond its use in capital crimes. Nearly half (46 percent) of prisoners in the state of Washington serving life without parole, for example, have been convicted of a non-homicide offense.[22] The rise in these sentences has significantly outpaced the decline in the death penalty as well as the rise in life sentences *with* the possibility of parole.

We can see this effect through the gross numbers of individuals serving life without parole sentences, currently 53,000; in the absence of a sentence of life without parole, it is inconceivable that more than a small fraction of this total would otherwise have been sentenced to death. Therefore, it logically follows that the vast majority of these individuals would formerly have been serving life sentences *with* the possibility of parole.

Disproportionate media attention on the death penalty in comparison to its relatively infrequent use could also explain the general public's lack of awareness about the extent to which life sentences are used, or even what a life sentence means in practice. The lack of focus on life sentences allows their numbers to expand with little notice or critique. A Texas study of jurors who served in capital murder trials found that they routinely underestimated the number of years to be served for a capital murder conviction in the absence of the death penalty, "with the average juror believing a person sentenced to life in prison will be paroled after 15 years."[23] In fact, the impetus for "truth-in-sentencing" laws derives partly from a sense that the public is being lied to in regard to the amount of time served in prison. Under Texas law at the time of the study, prisoners would have to serve a minimum of forty years before parole consideration.

Public polling indicates that most citizens believe that life sentences can be challenged as new evidence emerges. In a 2010 national public opinion poll, for example, respondents were asked to provide their level of agreement (on a scale of 0 to 10) with the following statement: *"With a sentence of life without parole, if new evidence of innocence emerges, the case can be reopened."* Sixty-six percent of respondents gave this a "10" and an additional 14 percent gave it an "8" or "9," meaning that the vast majority of respondents thought this was an option in life-sentenced cases.[24] Yet in reality this is rarely the case. Most states have time limits by which claims of innocence must be filed.[25] It is also more difficult to have a life without parole case examined because of the perception that less is at stake than with a death sentence. Over the past three decades, the opportunities for post-conviction appeals in the federal courts in particular have been drastically reduced.[26]

We count ourselves as dedicated members of the death penalty abolitionist community and therefore raise these questions in a spirit of challenge both to ourselves and to our colleagues. In the present political climate, a failure to support life without parole as an alternative to the death penalty in some cases will doom prospects for death penalty repeal. But if we hope to reach a point where this is not necessarily the case, we will need to explore strategies for communications and policy advocacy to deescalate punishments across the board.

This process will need to begin by challenging the identification of convicted individuals solely by their offense of conviction. Doing so risks cutting off any consideration of an individualized assessment of their life circumstances, capacity for change, or interventions in prison that could aid in such transformation. We have seen this shift in perspective with juvenile defendants, first with eliminating the death penalty as a sentencing option, followed by placing significant limitations on the use of life without parole. As noted, the Supreme Court sees juveniles as capable of change because of their stage of development. Yet while juveniles may be *uniquely* capable of change, so too are adults able to mature and transform their lives. The twenty-five-year-old convicted of murder in many cases will be a very different person by the age of forty. Recognizing these dynamics will help to shift the conversation about punishment from an offense-based response to a more individualized approach that takes into account both the offense and the individual.

Near-Term Reform Agenda

While establishing a twenty-year maximum prison term would produce better public safety outcomes, we recognize that such a shift in public policy will take time. But even as policymakers begin to consider changes to the sentencing structure, current sentencing and parole policies can be adjusted in myriad ways to produce better outcomes. The following recommendations provide a road map for those types of reforms.

Eliminate Life Without Parole Sentences

Even to the extent that policymakers are reluctant to reduce prison terms substantially, there is no justification for permitting the use of life without parole policies. As we have demonstrated, such sentences contribute little-to-no additional deterrent effect and in many cases result in prison terms well past the point of diminishing returns for public safety purposes. By denying hope to individuals who in many cases have made significant personal transformations, they are fundamentally inhumane.

The steady line of decisions from the U.S. Supreme Court in cases of juvenile life without parole illustrates the ways in which rational public policy can be developed. While the Court has largely based its decisions on the understanding that "children are different" in levels of maturity and culpability, such reasoning can also translate to adult defendants. Taking an individualized approach to sentencing, a process that is not currently possible in states that impose mandatory life without parole for certain offenses, allows for an investigation into life circumstances that can help us understand how criminal activity occurs. This is not meant to suggest that individuals are not responsible for their behavior, but rather that a broader understanding of these developments can aid in preventing future crimes. At the back end of the system, eliminating life without parole prison terms would not provide a guarantee of parole to any individual but would substantially reduce the degree of excessive sentencing that currently characterizes our prison system.

Eliminate Life Without Parole for Felony Murder

As a first step in a process of eliminating sentences of life without parole, policymakers should be reminded that the United States is unique among nations in treating accomplices to a felony that results in death as if they had committed the homicide themselves. A classic example of such a case would be the "getaway driver" waiting in a car outside a pharmacy where his companion kills the storeowner in the course of committing a robbery. Clearly, the accomplice needs to be held accountable for his role in the offense, but to impose the most severe penalty possible save a death sentence violates notions of fairness and proportionality.

Expedite Parole Eligibility: Establish a "Second Look" Policy

In a substantial number of states, the first opportunity for parole consideration comes after a much longer period of incarceration than is necessary to determine suitability for release, a trend that has been worsening in recent decades. As noted, for people serving long sentences the American Law Institute and other expert bodies have proposed an initial review, a "second look," to take place no later than fifteen years into the sentence. In addition, many states have extended the waiting period between parole hearings for those who are denied relief. This is unreasonable and doesn't permit timely recognition of personal transformation. Unless there are extenuating circumstances, subsequent parole hearings should be conducted on an annual basis.

Expand Prison Programming for Lifers

In many corrections systems, lifers have limited access to rehabilitative programming in prison. The rationale provided for this policy is generally that, since many lifers will never be released from prison (or at least not for several decades), it is not efficient to devote limited prison resources to them. Such a policy is both counterproductive and inhumane. For those lifers or long-term prisoners who will be eligible for parole consideration, programming in prison can both aid them in making transitions in their lives and also provide evidence to a parole board of their desire to lead a productive life.

Depoliticize and Professionalize the Parole Process

One of the many outcomes of the "get tough" era is that governors have frequently appointed parole board members based on their political connections rather than their expertise in clinical evaluation. Such decision-making only feeds into the "crime of the month" syndrome, by which political considerations outweigh clinical judgments in assessing the objectives of a parole system. Having psychological expertise on the parole board would empower paroling authorities to release individuals when they no longer pose an unreasonable risk to public safety.

Establish a Presumption of Parole

Rather than looking for failure or unduly focusing on the crime of conviction, parole boards should establish a presumption that an individual will be released after a specified period of time unless circumstances suggest otherwise. The release decision should be based on an assessment of the programmatic and disciplinary requirements established by the board, with latitude to extend the term of incarceration if public safety considerations override other factors.

Expand Compassionate Release

Dying in prison is an increasingly likely scenario for people serving life sentences. In many states, substantial numbers of people have served decades in prison and now present little threat for public safety because of their advanced age and/or development of serious, terminal illness. Yet these individuals have little opportunity for release except an extremely unlikely clemency grant. One way to express compassion for elderly individuals, as well as to curb the costs of the rising population of aging lifers, is to enhance opportunities for geriatric release. Such policies represent mechanisms that permit release from prison based on advanced age and/or chronic, terminal illness with almost no threat at all to public safety.

Statutes in forty-six states, the District of Columbia, and the federal government allow early release based on age and/or poor health. No such allowances are made for prisoners in Illinois, South Carolina, South Dakota, or Utah. Though compassionate release is a possibility in nearly all states, it is extremely rare for people serving life. In twenty-five states, early release of lifers for health or age-related reasons is eliminated for those with parole-ineligible sentences. In seven states, those with first- or second-degree murder convictions do not qualify. And in eleven states, crimes that are sexual in nature are ineligible for consideration.[27] States should eliminate offense-based restrictions on compassionate release and broaden its use overall.

Willis X. Harris

This is what Willis Harris wants you to know: "The general public has a lot of power they don't realize they have. They can demand changes in the criminal justice system by going to the legislature of the state they live in and demanding change. They can demand reconsideration or review of the lifer laws to facilitate release of deserving lifers. They can also question the governors about why he or she hasn't commuted the sentences of deserving lifers. And there are many deserving lifers who could be released today. Taxpayers put about $60 to $80 billion a year into the criminal justice system and get no return on their investment. Something needs to be done to reduce this mass incarceration, to release deserving people in prison who have been there for thirty, forty, and fifty years who pose no threat to public safety."

Willis speaks from experience. Retired since 2004, the seventy-nine-year-old Detroit native and resident once served as the director of community services for a private corrections agency and as a supervisor for a federal court community-based program providing services to probationers and parolees. That experience aside, Willis's credibility is bolstered by twenty-three and a half years in the Michigan prison system—from 1956 to 1980—sentenced to life without parole at age seventeen for a murder he maintains he did not commit. "I was accused of killing a woman in 1955 who I'd never met," he said in his gravelly, soft-spoken voice. "I told the court I never committed the crime and I never learned who the victim is. They laughed at me, and I was sentenced to prison for the rest of my life."

A good student, Willis Harris graduated from high school at sixteen and went to work as a stock clerk for a local retailer. Earning his own money, he said, eased the burden on his hard-working parents. "It's how I was raised." But before he turned seventeen, he was arrested at his workplace and charged with murder. "One of the officers told me that they had a lot of cold cases that had been unsolved too long, and it was time to solve some of them and they would start with me."

The African American son of working-class parents, he grew up in a tight, culturally mixed neighborhood despite segregation being the law of the land in 1950s America. "My life was pretty normal. There was some segregated places then, but in my community, everyone got along with each other. You could leave your door unlocked at night. People cross-associated, they thought nothing of it."

But the Detroit criminal justice system lacked the same sense of convergence. "If you were black and the victim was Caucasian, even if you told the truth it had no relevance. No significance at all because Caucasian police officers didn't lie. Only black people lied," Willis recalled, adding that in some cities and jurisdictions little has changed. "We had a prejudiced police department, a prejudiced newspaper, and a prejudiced jury. My trial lasted one week, but it took twenty-five minutes for the jury to find me guilty of murder."

Driven by the judge's pronouncement, seventeen-year-old Willis was determined that the sentence of "life without parole" would not be the final word. Maintaining his innocence and a strong sense of righteous determination, he immersed himself in nearly every training and rehabilitation opportunity the Michigan Department of Corrections made available to prisoners. In his time, people serving life could participate in any number of programs or courses, such as financial and nursing classes, teacher training, first aid, and public speaking. He says this kind of programming today is virtually nonexistent for lifers with or without parole and sorely lacking for all prisoners. "It was better then. There were more programs for lifers. The governors and parole boards were commuting mandatory lifers. And they don't return," he said, referring to the impressive statistics about lifer recidivism that show them to be the lowest risk, by a wide margin, of any class of prisoner. "That was true then and it holds true today."

The classes Willis took while incarcerated benefited him after prison. Assigned to several facilities—Jackson, Ionia, Marquette, Camp Raymond—he worked as a teacher's aide, psychiatric nurse's aide, clerk, general assistant, and prison newspaper editor. "I did very little time in my cell. Most of the jobs they gave me had me out sometimes until midnight. I always had jobs. You got your job based on your crime, education, and IQ." For years he was part of the trusty program, his last two at Camp Raymond where he worked as the clerk, general assistant, and camp nurse. "There were no fences, no walls, no locked doors, no guards walking around there," he said. "I had three jobs working directly for the regional supervisor."

He also started the first Lifers Association in the Michigan Department of Corrections. "We had about three thousand lifers in prison during the seventies, most with and some without parole. The prison had an organization called Prisoner's Progress Association, which did nothing. I proposed we start a lifers committee and people liked that idea." But Willis was concerned that the committee would be just another do-nothing group if run by the Prisoner's Progress leadership, so he insisted that if he started it, he would run it. "I wouldn't let them use it to attack the corrections department. That's not what the group was going to be about. We were about improving things for lifers. So I asked the warden for permission to run it independently, and he approved it." With Willis at the head, the group picked its own members, refusing to let malcontents and troublemakers join. "We had ten people: five Caucasians, four blacks, and one Hispanic. It was a pretty good group. I ran it until I was released in 1980. I don't know what happened, but after an incident when a female officer was raped and killed in that prison, everything was shut down, all the programs they had for prisoners. They closed them down statewide."

Despite his exemplary record, the road to freedom for Willis Harris was mined with obstacles beyond his life without parole sentence. In 1978, he appeared before the parole board on his request for commutation. He received a favorable recommendation which was then sent to the governor's office. But his accomplishments and jobs, particularly as editor of the prison newspaper, had bred animosity and resentment from some prison guards. While editor of *The Spectator*, the paper at Jackson Correctional Facility, Willis had articles published in the local paper, the *Jackson Citizen-Patriot*, contradicting what he called misleading stories about prison conditions and programs. As a result, his movements around the trusty division were restricted, and he earned the ire of prison officials.

"Two inmates, for whatever reason, put a false charge against me for obtaining money from the state under false pretenses. My case was removed from the governor's office until the conclusion of the investigation." After more than a year, he was cleared of any wrongdoing. His recommendation reinstated, then-Michigan governor William Milliken commuted Willis's life sentence, and he was paroled on June 4, 1980.

Willis continues to advocate for criminal justice reform, though now as a volunteer. He works with nonprofit agencies to help connect formerly incarcerated persons with needed services for housing, employment, and treatment and is involved with advocacy groups working to pass legislation on sentencing reform and post-release support services. In keeping with his prison journalism roots, he also publishes two newsletters about lifers, a task he takes great pride in doing.

About three years ago Willis received a call from Charles Sullivan, the national president of CURE, a national prison reform organization. "They had a newsletter, but the editor died. They had no one out here to take charge of it. [Sullivan] asked me if I would be the director of the *CURE Lifelong* newsletter. I'd never met him in person, he must have got my name from somebody." The newsletter's editor is a prisoner in Massachusetts, Willis said, who sends it to him for review and approval. "I have it printed and distributed. It's about issues that affect lifers and other virtual lifers, people whose sentences start at fifty years or more."

Working with the CURE newsletter led Willis to starting his own publication, the *Michigan Lifers Report*. "I've got now about fifty subscribers. This newsletter, I started it sometime last year, though it's been on my mind for a long time. We collect information to inform the public and lifers about what they need to know. We let the prisoners write their stories, we write stories based on our experience, and we also report information on lifer law changes across the country and we encourage the inmates to write articles based on their experiences and how it affects their families."

Always the advocate for lifers, Willis speaks regularly at colleges, at high schools, on radio programs, and to civic organizations about criminal justice issues. "People are told everyone is the worst of the worst. It's how politicians report on criminal justice, how the media reports on criminal justice. Nothing is said about the person twenty or thirty years later, when they change their lives and are rehabilitated and are no risk to anyone. They want to hide that from the public, they want people to believe that once a killer, always a killer; once a drug dealer, always a drug dealer; once a robber, always a robber. They want the public to believe that they can never be anything else."

As for better conditions for lifers in his state of Michigan, Willis dismisses recent legislation as cosmetic paperwork. In practice, he says, programs are designed for those with parole dates, not for those without any potential for parole. Lifers are at the bottom of the list. "They got some makeshift programs for short timers that are ineffective, janitorial and cooking. But training for jobs that are needed today in society, they don't have them. Not even for short timers."

Willis Harris's personal transformation is not atypical, and he knows it. His life after incarceration has been a living example. As he approaches his thirty-ninth year post-prison, he wishes the policymakers and the public would know it too.

The Future of Life in America

For the nation that leads the world in incarceration, that is virtually the only industrialized nation still maintaining the death penalty, and that uses life imprisonment to a remarkable degree, it may seem audacious to propose to scale back maximum sentences to twenty years. But the goal of a twenty-year maximum sentence may not be as farfetched as one might think. Several recent social movements have demonstrated the ability of organizing campaigns to gain traction and support for ideas and policies once considered to be at the fringe of political discussion.

The campaign for same-sex marriage, culminating in the U.S. Supreme Court *Obergefell* decision in 2015, was remarkable in a nation where Americans were opposed to same-sex marriage by 57 to 35 percent in a 2001 Pew Research Center survey, and where thirty-nine states as late as 2010 still maintained marriage bans. While the years leading up to the decision seemed to reflect a rapidly changing political environment, the campaign was in fact an outgrowth of decades of strategizing and organizing. The victory in the Supreme Court was shaped by initial victories at the state and local levels, by the bold campaigns for recognition by the gay community, and by the courage of millions of Americans coming out to their friends and families.

The Occupy movement demonstrated the power of a strong message linked to local and national visibility, all building on recognition of growing inequality in America. Who would have thought that a relative handful of mostly youthful protestors in a New York City park could arouse a degree of passion that would lead national political figures to embrace their call to support "the 99 percent"?

We have also witnessed the surge of the Black Lives Matter movement, born out of decades of frustration and outrage at police tactics in African American communities. Here, too, what may have seemed on the surface to be a response to the tragic events in Ferguson, Baltimore, Staten Island, Cleveland, and elsewhere, was instead an expression of decades-long resentment of a police presence more frequently perceived as hostile to their communities than guardians of their public safety.

In addition to sending a powerful message regarding gender relations and abuse, the #MeToo movement has produced short-term results that would have seemed unimaginable just a few years ago. With scores of men in influential positions in media, popular culture, and politics being forced to acknowledge their crimes and misconduct, we have yet to assess the full potential of this movement to shift cultural assumptions and power relations over time.

What these movements have in common is that they have shaped the national conversation around a range of issues once considered to be primarily the provenance of interest groups without a large organized constituency. In so doing, they have placed pressure on political leadership, media, and institutions to recognize and respond to deep-seated and widely shared grievances.

Against this background we see the potential of a campaign to challenge the use of life sentences, to advocate for a twenty-year maximum penalty, and to strive for a more rational, fair, and humane approach to criminal justice across the board in America. Such a campaign does not need to be created in a vacuum, but rather can build on the momentum for criminal justice reform of the past decade.

The climate for justice reform is now substantially different from that of the "war on crime" decades that persisted until the early

2000s. In addition to the Black Lives Matter movement, we have seen the expansion of state and local campaigns focused around halting prison expansion and the use of private prisons, promoting the right to vote for people with felony convictions, challenging the racial bias of criminal justice policy and practice, and calling attention to "crimmigration," the growing intersection of immigration enforcement and criminal justice processing.

Practitioners in many fields within the criminal justice system have come to embrace strategic shifts in how they do their work and think about their goals. Corrections leaders in almost every state have embraced the concept of reentry, the need to structure the process of people returning home to their communities following incarceration into a positive experience designed to encourage success, not a return to prison. Court systems now routinely employ programs to divert individuals with substance abuse problems into treatment programs as a first step, rather than imprisonment. And even given the critique of law enforcement practices, there has been a growing movement to define and embrace the concept of community policing in which strategies and tactics are designed to encourage cooperation, not conflict, between law enforcement and the communities they police.

In far too many cases, the pace of change or quantity of resources devoted to new initiatives is too modest to produce any substantial shift in outcomes. Many observers have also pointed out the risk of "widening the net" of social control through the use of "alternatives" that too often function as expansions of the system, not as alternative means of resolving conflict.

Despite important questions about both the pace and the scale of the reform movement, the momentum for criminal justice reform has begun to transform the political environment on criminal justice policy in important ways. Much of this activity has translated to significant policy change at the state level. Since 2000, at least twenty-nine states have enacted some type of reform to their mandatory sentencing policies, and ten states have reduced their prison populations by at least 15 percent.

At the federal level, even with an overly partisan Congress, criminal justice reform has emerged as one of the few issues capable of producing agreement across the aisle. In 2010, Congress enacted the Fair Sentencing Act, which reduced the notorious disparity in sentencing between crack cocaine and powder cocaine. In a series of policy shifts the U.S. Sentencing Commission lowered its drug sentencing guidelines, leading to reduced prison terms for thousands of people in federal prisons. And each year legislators now approve funding for reentry programming and justice reinvestment support to aid local communities in addressing public safety in ways that don't rely on harsh punishments.

Perhaps most notably, in President Obama's last years in office he ramped up the executive clemency process substantially. By the end of his tenure Obama had commuted the sentences of 1,715 individuals, of whom nearly a third were serving life sentences for drug offenses.

Among them was Norman Brown, imprisoned for his role in a crack cocaine drug conspiracy. Brown had grown up in a solid middle-class home; his father worked for the Marriott Corporation, his mother was a school teacher, and he aspired to go to college. But during the 1980s rise of crack cocaine, high-level drug sellers began to sport fancy cars and clothing, and Norman Brown was one of the many young men attracted by that lifestyle. In 1993, he was convicted of being part of a drug ring in which the FBI charged that he and a co-conspirator were moving five kilograms of crack cocaine weekly. Because Brown had two prior drug convictions, he was sentenced under a mandatory third strike provision and sentenced to life without parole at the age of twenty-four.

While in prison Brown engaged in a broad range of activities— he became a vegetarian and engaged in anger management classes, self-help groups, and sports, never giving up hope for his free-dom. After filing a clemency request in 2014 he finally succeeded in obtaining a commutation from President Obama in 2016 after twenty-four years of incarceration. Today he is a valued staff member of Project New Opportunity in Washington, DC, a nonprofit organization that provides support to individuals returning home from federal prisons.

The public environment for a reconsideration of life-long sentences has shifted remarkably: bestselling books of recent years, including *The New Jim Crow*, Michelle Alexander's racial critique of mass incarceration, and *Just Mercy*, Bryan Stevenson's powerful call for compassion for his clients on death row and in the bowels of the justice system, have helped to shift public opinion.[1] Likewise, Ava DuVernay's Oscar-nominated *13th* provides the narrative tracing the racial antecedents of mass incarceration over the course of two centuries that has heightened awareness of racial disparities in the criminal justice system.[2]

None of this suggests that achieving the goal of a twenty-year maximum prison term will be easy. But criminal justice reform has never been easy. From the days of hellhole prisons like Attica, to the various "wars on drugs" over the past century, to the modern-day inception of three-strikes laws and the state-sanctioned execution of people by lethal injections, reformers have had to struggle to maintain a vision for reform that is premised on both evidence and compassion.

Many of those campaigns have achieved success in calling public attention to the grave injustices being inflicted on our fellow citizens and in securing changes in how the justice system works. The current challenge is equally formidable, but we take it on with lessons learned over many decades and buoyed by a growing demand for change.

Fundamentally, Americans need to ask ourselves what type of

society we wish to live in. Despite the progress we have made, we are nonetheless defined as a nation by centuries of racism, growing inequality, and extreme punishment. Ending life imprisonment would constitute a major step toward making us a more just and humane society.

Author's Note

Four decades ago I made the first of what would become my many visits to Jackson Prison in Michigan. Officially known as the State Prison of Southern Michigan, "Jackson" was known to the tens of thousands of people who passed through it as the largest walled prison in the world. Originally constructed in 1839, and with additions over many decades, the prison came to house six thousand people by the 1970s.

For someone like me who had at the time only modest experience inside penal institutions, entering the prison grounds felt like a scene straight out of Hollywood. Enclosed by a 33-foot-high concrete wall topped with barbed wire and armed staff in a dozen guard towers, the massive structure was foreboding. Entering the reception area for visitors brought little comfort. A grimy and noisy reception room was filled mostly with family members waiting for the call to see their loved ones, who were being tracked down in the massive institution and given permission to head down to the visiting room. I dutifully presented my identification, signed in, deposited the contents of my pockets in a locker, and sat down to wait my turn.

I was at Jackson as a young staffer of the American Friends Service Committee, the Quaker social justice organization, where I had begun working on criminal justice reform issues under the tutelage of Barbara Cartwright. During the year I first visited Jackson I had read an intriguing book of correspondence between a leftist

author, Ethel Shapiro-Bertolini, and a number of incarcerated individuals. One of the most prolific writers in the group was Ronnie
Irwin, then housed at Jackson Prison. His correspondence with the
author involved a years-long debate and discussion on the meaning
of social change, strategies for reform, and life in prison. I wrote
to Ms. Shapiro-Bertolini, and she put me in touch with Irwin, who
by then had taken the name Ahmad Rahman. He subsequently
invited me to visit him at the prison.

Rahman was then in his late twenties and was serving a sentence of life without parole for a crime committed as an outgrowth
of his political engagement. After becoming radicalized through
the civil rights and anti-war movements of the 1960s, he had joined
the Black Panther Party in his hometown of Chicago. Several years
later he relocated to Detroit, aligning with the Panther chapter
there.

At the time the Black Panther Party took a hard line on drugs in
the black community. Viewing drugs, and drug sellers, as a scourge
on the community, the organization regularly hosted rallies and
engaged in public education on the harm that drugs brought to the
cause of black liberation.

On occasion, this activism became much more confrontational
in its efforts to drive drug purveyors out of the community. Thus,
in 1971 Ahmad Rahman and three other Panthers staged a raid on
a student commune in Detroit that they believed was a heroin den.
While Rahman was on the second floor of the house, one of his
accomplices shot and killed an occupant on the first floor.

All four of the home invaders were apprehended and had charges
filed against them. The other three Panthers agreed to take a plea
in return for a reduced prison term. The "triggerman" subsequently
served twelve years in prison before being paroled.

Rahman chose to go to trial, charged with felony murder. As
is true in virtually every state, felony murder statutes essentially

equate participation in a felony resulting in a murder with actually committing the murder.

Ahmad Rahman was found guilty of felony murder and sentenced to life without parole. Such a sentence means exactly what it sounds like, a sentence that would culminate in death in prison.

My visit with Ahmad became the first in a decades-long friendship that taught me a lot about prison, Islam, black political engagement, and many other issues. At one visit we chatted about Ahmad's hosting a jazz show on the prison radio station. He would play selections from Miles, Coltrane, and others and offer political commentary in between. But why did the prison officials condone the political conversation? I wondered. Apparently, they were largely unaware of it. Referring to the primarily rural white prison guards, Ahmad noted that "They hate our music, and we hate their music." There wasn't much cross-pollination going on between the jazz and country aficionados.

Although Ahmad was engaged in constructive programming while incarcerated and was well-respected in the institution, he still had no legal right to parole consideration. The only possible form of release for someone with that status would be clemency from the governor, an act that is rarely employed in most states.

Nonetheless, a broad range of outside supporters who had come to know Ahmad rallied around him in a campaign for gubernatorial action. Key sponsors included Jim Ricci, a widely read columnist in the major state newspaper, the *Detroit Free Press*, and Detroit mayor Coleman Young. Following high-level coverage of the case, and with broad support from the community, Republican governor John Engler granted a commutation of sentence in 1992, after twenty-one years of incarceration.

Freedom granted Ahmad intellectual and social opportunity, which he jumped at. Building on his interest in African history, he gained admission to the graduate program at the University of

Michigan's Department of Afroamerican and African Studies and several years later was awarded his doctorate. He then joined the faculty of the University of Michigan-Dearborn campus, and I still recall with great joy the day he called to tell me he had just been granted tenure. In 2013 Ahmad was recognized as College Professor of the Year by the Michigan Council for the Social Studies.

During his time at the university Ahmad was heavily engaged in community outreach, much of it focused on providing support for children without a father in the home. He was fond of saying that in his youth he had been a *revolutionary* but had since become a *solutionary*. Sadly, he died of a sudden heart attack at the age of sixty-four, having used his years of freedom in service to the community.

Over time I came to know many other lifers at Jackson, largely through connecting with an organized advocacy group, the National Lifers of America (NLA). The NLA consisted of a group of men in their thirties and forties, typically serving life for either murder or robbery. Many had been in their late teens or early twenties when they committed their crimes, frequently related to being engaged in illegal activities involving drugs, theft, and other offenses.

By the time I got to know them, they were very different people than the younger versions of themselves that they described to me. Like teenagers on the outside, they had matured over the years, in many cases becoming very thoughtful and compassionate, and even displaying a keen sense of humor within the confines of the prison system.

Most of the men expressed remorse for their actions and recognized why they were being punished. But they also expressed frustration that they had no means of expressing that remorse in any meaningful sense because the justice system made no provision for that type of restoration.

One of the men once asked me to obtain contact information for

Save the Children, the international organization providing support to children in need around the world. I was happy to do so and asked what he needed it for. He was employed in the prison kitchen, earning less than one dollar an hour, but still ending up with a bit of money at the end of the month even after making his commissary purchases. He told me he wanted to send five dollars a month to the organization, as a small way of paying his debt to society.

It's true, of course, that the men in the NLA group may have been among the more introspective of the lifer population, or the ones who had made the most significant internal transformations. And whether inside prison or on the outside, all of us know many adults who still "act like children" from time to time, or seem to have missed some of the pathways to adulthood. So we know that not everyone in prison has "aged out" of crime by the age of forty or fifty. But many have, and in far too many cases the prison system has no means of recognizing this transformation and reconsidering the wisdom of a life sentence.

Over the years I've thought of my lifer contacts frequently and have been able to keep up with a number of them. A handful were paroled over time. Some did remarkably well adjusting back to the community, but many struggled. All of the disadvantages and disabilities that accompany someone with a felony conviction are in full bloom for those generally identified solely by the crime they committed. Not to mention a couple of decades behind bars, with little to show given the limited availability of job training or educational programming for lifers in prison.

As I transitioned to The Sentencing Project and began to author a series of publications examining trends in the use of incarceration, I noticed over time that there was rarely any discussion, or even available data, on the number of people serving life prison terms.

In part to satisfy my curiosity and in part because of the dearth of policy discussion on lifers, I initially embarked on life imprisonment research to obtain basic estimates of the number of such cases. My colleagues Ryan King and Malcolm Young and I produced a report on the number of people serving such sentences in 2004. I know a fair amount about criminal justice data but was nonetheless shocked to find that 127,000 individuals were serving life sentences—one of every eleven people in prison.

Since then my colleague and co-author Ashley Nellis has headed up our research initiative in this area, with three subsequent analyses of this trend data. One of her reports followed the U.S. Supreme Court decision in the case of *Miller v. Alabama*, which barred the mandatory application of life without parole to juveniles.

Ashley had suggested to me that a next stage of understanding the experience of life imprisonment would be to conduct a survey of the approximately 2,500 individuals serving these sentences for crimes committed when they were under the age of eighteen. I proceeded to tell her why that would be a bad idea. It's always problematic dealing with mail going in and out of prisons. Many of these people have never filled out a survey, so they would be confused about how to do so. Literacy rates are low among people in prison, so that would affect the response rate. And so on.

But Ashley talked me into it, and I'm grateful that she did. We sent her fifteen-page survey to as many of the 2,500 as we could contact (only prisoners in Louisiana were excluded, and this was for litigation-based reasons) and received a remarkable 68 percent response rate. The findings of that survey were both enlightening and disturbing, and are described in this volume. Perhaps the most poignant aspect of this project was the volume of phone calls and messages we received from family members of the incarcerated individuals. Many were calling just to let us know that their loved one had received the survey and was working on it. Others sought assistance and information in trying to interpret the implications of the Supreme Court decision. And some just expressed their gratitude that someone cared enough to ask them about their experiences.

As we hope we have documented in this book, for reasons of compassion, public safety, and addressing the twenty-first-century nightmare of mass incarceration, we need to think and act more on the dramatic numbers of people serving life imprisonment in the United States. Along with virtually every other element of our criminal justice system, it casts a stain on our democracy and places us far out of line with comparable nations. It is long past time to confront these challenges.

—Marc Mauer

Acknowledgments

This book would not have been published without the support and encouragement of the staff at The New Press over many years. Thanks in particular to Diane Wachtell for her persistence in telling us that "we need a good book on life imprisonment," and we hope this is that book. And thanks to Diane and to Jed Bickman for editing and logistical support, as well as to all our colleagues at The New Press who labor to produce a great collection of books for the world we live in today.

The Meaning of Life grows out of our work at The Sentencing Project over many years and in particular from more than a decade's worth of research and thinking about life imprisonment. In doing this work we've had the support of a board of directors who provide us with just the right mix of wisdom and passion for justice in their stewardship of the organization. We've also been fortunate to be aided by a talented and enthusiastic staff who share our commitment to social justice. Thanks in particular to Jessica Yoo for her copious research and citations support, to Casey Anderson for research assistance, to Morgan McLeod for editorial and logistics support, and to Nazgol Ghandnoosh for review and editing.

Our deep appreciation to the individuals who opened up their lives and experiences with life imprisonment to our readers: Anita Colon, Denise Dodson, Kelly Garrett, Willis X. Harris, Robert Holbrook, Sam Lewis, Justin Singleton, and William Underwood. We appreciate their courage in sharing their stories of both pain and transformation. And our gratitude to our colleague Kerry Myers for his strength and perseverance and for the impact of his journalism in telling stories of prison and life sentences over many years.

We could not have accomplished as much as we have over three decades without the support of our funders at every level. To the foundations large and small who have understood our mission and given us the flexibility to act strategically, thanks so much. And for the thousands of individual donors large and small who connected with us through their financial support, please know that this work could not happen without you.

Over many years we've been stimulated and supported by colleagues in the field who are engaged on these issues as researchers, policymakers, practitioners, and advocates. Our proposal in the book for a twenty-year cap on prison terms builds on the work of scholars including Todd Clear, Jonathan Simon, and Michael Tonry, who have made compelling arguments over many years regarding the excessive nature of punishment in the United States. For international insight we've benefited greatly from discussions with Dirk van Zyl Smit and Catherine Appleton. We express great appreciation to Jeffrey Hantover for his sharp editing eye, to Richard Frase and Robert Johnson for chapter reviews, and to Jeremy Travis for stimulating our thinking on issues of life imprisonment. Bob Brown and John Braithwaite have provided insight into lifer programming in Canada, as has Timothy Head in the United States.

And, of course, we thank our networks of family and friends who have provided both enthusiastic support for this undertaking as well as pleasant diversions from it.

Notes

Introduction: Lessons of "The Birdman"

1. "Robert 'The Birdman of Alcatraz' Stroud," Famous Inmates, Alcatraz History, http://www.alcatrazhistory.com/stroud.htm.

2. Ashley Nellis, "Still Life: America's Increasing Use of Life and Long-Term Sentences" (The Sentencing Project, 2017).

Life by the Numbers

1. Kathleen Maguire, Ann L. Pastore, and Timothy Flanagan (eds.), *Sourcebook of Criminal Justice Statistics 1992* (Washington, DC: Bureau of Justice Statistics, 1993).

2. Dirk van Zyl Smit and Catherine Appleton, *Life Imprisonment: A Global Human Rights Analysis* (Cambridge, MA: Harvard University Press, forthcoming, 2018).

3. Catherine Appleton and Dirk van Zyl Smit, *Challenging Life Imprisonment* (2018), available at: https://www.compen.crim.cam.ac.uk/Blog/blog-pages-full-versions/guest-blog-on-challenging-life-imprisonment.

4. In capital cases where the death penalty is sought and not chosen, states typically default to mandatory life without parole.

5. Elizabeth Dermody Leonard, *Convicted Survivors: The Imprisonment of Battered Women* (Albany, NY: SUNY Press, 2002).

6. Judith Haley, "A Study of Women Imprisoned for Homicide, Georgia Department of Corrections," June 1992.

7. Michigan Battered Women's Clemency Project, *Clemency for Battered Women in Michigan: A Manual for Attorneys, Law Students and Social Workers*, available online at http://www.umich.edu/~clemency/clemency_manual/manual_intro.html.

8. Leonard, *Convicted Survivors*.

Policies That Drive Life Sentences

1. "Sentencing in Utah," Utah Board of Pardons and Paroles, Accessed January 19, 2018, www.bop.utah.gov.

2. David M. Zlotnick, "The Future of Federal Sentencing Policy: Learning Lessons from Republican Judicial Appointees in the Guidelines Era," *University of Colorado Law Review*, 79 no. 1 (2007): 1–76.

3. "Attorney General Holder Delivers Remarks at the Annual Meeting of the American Bar Association's House of Delegates," U.S. Department of Justice, Accessed January 18, 2018, http://www.justice.gov/iso/opa/ag/speeches /2013/ag-speech-130812.html.

4. Barbara Levine, *The High Cost of Denying Parole: An Analysis of Prisoners Eligible for Release* (Lansing, MI: Citizens Alliance on Prisons and Public Spending, November, 2003), 31.

5. Baldwin v. Tennessee Board of Paroles No. M2002-01428-COA-R3-CV (2003).

6. Nazgol Ghandnoosh "Delaying a Second Chance: The Declining Prospects for Parole on Life Sentences," Washington, DC: The Sentencing Project (2017): 17–18, accessed January 18, 2018, http://www.sentencingproject .org/wp-content/uploads/2017/01/Delaying-a-Second-Chance.pdf.

7. Ghandnoosh, "Delaying a Second Chance," 17–18.

8. Alexis Lee Watts, Kevin R. Reitz, Edward E. Rhine, and Mariel E. Alper, *Profiles in Parole Release and Revocation in Georgia* (Minneapolis: Robina Institute of Criminal Law and Criminal Justice, 2016).

9. Molly Gill, "Clemency for Lifers: The Only Road Out Is the Road Not Taken," *Federal Sentencing Reporter* 23, no. 1 (2010): 21–26.

10. "Application for Commutation of Life Sentences." Pennsylvania Board of Pardons, accessed January 4, 2018: http://www.bop.pa.gov/Statistics /Pages/Commutation-of-Life-Sentences.aspx.

11. Mark Hollis, "Florida Toughest on Teen Criminals," *Sun Sentinel*, 2000, accessed January 18, 2018, http://articles.sun-sentinel.com/2000-05 -18/news/0005180020_1_juvenile-crime-mandatory-minimum-sentences -jeb-bush.

Doing Life

1. Ben Crewe, "Depth, Weight, Tightness: Revisiting the Pains of Imprisonment," *Punishment and Society* 13, no. 5 (2011): 509–29; Timothy Flanagan, "Dealing with Long-Term Confinement: Adaptive Strategies and Perspectives Among Long-Term Prisoners," *Criminal Justice and Behavior* 8, no. 2 (June 1981): 201–22; Elisa Toman, Joshua C. Cochran, John K. Cochran,

and William D. Bales, "The Implications of Sentence Length for Inmate Adjustment to Prison Life," *Journal of Criminal Justice* 43 (2015): 510–21.

2. Marieke Liem, *After Life Imprisonment: Reentry in the Age of Mass Incarceration* (New York: New York University Press, 2017), 48.

3. Daniel P. LeClair and Susan Guarino-Ghezzi, "Does Incapacitation Guarantee Public Safety? Lessons from the Massachusetts Furlough and Prerelease Programs," *Justice Quarterly* 8, no. 1 (1991): 9–36.

4. Lisa Lorant and Robert Tenaglia, *1988 Annual Statistical Report of the Furlough Program*, Massachusetts Department of Correction (1989).

5. Timothy Flanagan, "Long-Term Incarceration: Issues of Science, Policy, Correctional Practice," in *Long-Term Incarceration: Issues of Science, Policy, Correctional Practice*, ed. Timothy Flanagan (Thousand Oaks, CA: Sage, 1995), 3.

6. Ashley Nellis, *The Lives of Juvenile Lifers: A National Portrait* (Washington, DC: The Sentencing Project, 2012).

7. Lila Kazemian and Jeremy Travis, "Imperative for Inclusion of Long Termers and Lifers in Research and Policy," *Criminology and Public Policy* 14, no. 2 (2014): 355–95.

8. Flanagan, "Long-Term Incarceration," 3–9; Kazemian and Travis, "Imperative for Inclusion."

9. Steve Herbert, "Inside or Outside? Expanding the Narratives About Life-Sentenced Prisoners," *Punishment and Society*, online first (October 2017).

10. Hans Toch, *Living in Prison: The Ecology of Survival* (New York: Free Press, 1977); Robert Johnson, Anne Marie Rocheleau, and Alison B. Martin, *Hard Time: A Free Look at Understanding and Reforming the Prison* (Hoboken, NJ: Wiley-Blackwell, 2016); Shadd Maruna, *Making Good: How Ex-Convicts Reform and Rebuild Their Lives* (Washington, DC: American Psychological Association, 2000); Marieke Liem, *After Life Imprisonment*; Margaret Leigey, *The Forgotten Men: Serving a Life without Parole Sentence* (New Brunswick, NJ; Rutgers University Press, 2015).

11. Gresham Sykes, *The Society of Captives* (Princeton, NJ: Princeton University Press, 1958).

12. Toman, "The Implications of Sentencing Length for Adjustment to Prison Life."

13. Johnson, *Hard Time*.

14. Johnson, *Hard Time*.

15. Kazemian and Travis, "Imperative for Inclusion."

16. Maruna, *Making Good*.

17. David Patrick Connor and Richard Tewksbury, "Prison Inmates and Their Visitors: An Examination of Inmate Characteristics and Visitor Types," *Prison Journal* 59 (2015): 159–77; James Patrick Lynch and William Sabol, *Prisoner Reentry in Perspective* (Washington, DC: Urban Institute, 2001); Michael Massoglia, Brianna Remster, and Ryan D. King "Stigma or Separation? Understanding the Incarceration-Divorce Relationship," *Social Forces* 90 (2011): 133–55.

18. Margaret Leigey and K. L. Reed, "A Woman's Life Before Serving Life: Examining the Negative Pre-Incarceration Life Events of Female Life-Sentenced Inmates," *Women and Criminal Justice* 20, no. 4 (2010): 302–22.

19. Liem, *After Life Imprisonment*, 75.

20. National Research Council, *The Growth of Incarceration in the United States: Exploring Causes and Consequences* (Washington, DC: The National Academies Press, 2014).

21. Meredith Huey Dye, Ronald Aday, Lori Farney, and Jordan Raley, "'The Rock I Cling To': Religious Engagement in the Lives of Life-Sentenced Women, *Prison Journal* 94 (2014): 388–408; Marieke Liem and MJ Kunst, "Is There a Recognizable Post-Incarceration Syndrome Among Released 'Lifers'?" *International Journal of Law and Psychiatry* 36, nos. 3–4 (2013): 333–37.

22. Sarah Mehta, *False Hope: How Parole Systems Fail Youth Serving Extreme Sentences* (Washington, DC: American Civil Liberties Union, 2016).

23. Liem, *After Life Imprisonment*.

24. Bruce Western, "Stress and Hardship After Prison," *American Journal of Sociology* 120, no. 5 (March 2015): 1512–47.

25. Flanagan, "Long-Term Confinement."

26. Liem and Kunst, "Post-Incarceration Syndrome," 336.

27. Liem, *After Life Imprisonment*.

"Death Is Different"

1. Furman v. Georgia, 408 U.S. 238 (1972), at 309.

2. Gregg v. Georgia, 428 U.S. 153 (1976).

3. Woodson v. North Carolina, 428 U.S. 280 (1976).

4. Rummel v. Estelle, 445 U.S. 263 (1980).

5. *Rummel* 445 U.S. at 276.

6. Harmelin v. Michigan, 501 U.S. 957 (1991).

7. Linda Greenhouse, "The Winds of Change," *New York Times*, September 18, 2013.

8. Ewing v. California, 538 U.S. 11 (2003).

9. Solem v. Helm, 463 U.S. 277.

10. Glen Campbell v. Ohio, 583 U.S. ___ (2018).

11. Rachel E. Barkow, "Life Without Parole and the Hope for Real Sentencing Reform," in *Life without Parole: America's New Death Penalty,* ed. Charles Ogletree and Austin Sarat (New York: New York University Press, 2012), 190–226.

12. Graham v. Florida, 560 U.S. 48 (2010).

13. Paolo Annino, David Rasmussen, and Chelsea Boehme, "Juvenile Life Without Parole for Nonhomicide Offenses: Florida Compared to the Nation" (Tallahassee, FL: Public Interest Law Center, 2009).

14. State v. Castaneda, 889 NW 2d 87 (2017).

15. Commonwealth v. Cunningham, No. 38 EAP (2012).

16. Montgomery v. Louisiana, 136 S. Ct. 718 (2016).

17. Amnesty International, "Death Sentences and Executions, 2016" (London: Amnesty International, 2017).

18. Carol S. Steiker and Jordan M. Steiker, *Courting Death: The Supreme Court and Capital Punishment* (Boston: Harvard University Press, 2017).

The American Commitment to Punishment

1. State v. Gwynne, 2017 Ohio 7570.

2. Roy Walmsley, "World Prison Brief" (London: Institute for Criminal Policy Research, 2016).

3. National Research Council, *The Growth of Incarceration in the United States: Exploring Causes and Consequences* (Washington, DC: The National Academies Press, 2014).

4. James Q. Whitman, *Harsh Justice: Criminal Punishment and the Widening Divide Between America and Europe* (New York: Oxford University Press, 2003).

5. Anthony N. Doob and Cheryl Marie Webster, "Creating the Will to Change: The Challenges of Mass Incarceration," *Criminology and Public Policy* 13, no. 4 (2014): 547–99.

6. AP, "Gravely Ill, Atwater Offers Apology," *New York Times,* January 13, 1991.

7. Jane Gross, "Born of Grief, 'Three Strikes' Laws Are Being Rethought," *New York Times,* December 2, 2013.

8. Michael Tonry, "Race, Ethnicity, Crime, and Immigration," in *Ethnicity, Crime, and Immigration: Comparative and Cross-National Perspectives,* ed. Michael Tonry (Chicago: University of Chicago Press Journals, 1996).

9. David J. Rothman, "Perfecting the Prison: United States, 1789–1865," in *The Oxford History of the Prison: The Practice of Punishment in Western*

Society, eds. Norval Morris and David J. Rothman (New York: Oxford University Press, 1995), 116–19.

10. David M. Oshinsky, *Worse Than Slavery: Parchman Farm and the Ordeal of Jim Crow Justice* (New York: Free Press, 1996).

11. Oshinsky, *Worse Than Slavery*.

12. New York Civil Liberties Union, "Stop-and-Frisk Data" (New York Civil Liberties Union, 2017).

13. Floyd v. City of New York, 813 F. Supp. 2d 417 (S.D.N.Y. 2011).

14. Marc Mauer, "The Endurance of Racial Disparity in the Criminal Justice System," in *Policing the Black Man*, ed. Angela J. Davis (New York: Pantheon Books, 2017), 34.

The Meaning of Life Around the World

1. *Vinter and others v. United Kingdom*, European Court of Human Rights, July 9, 2013.

2. Roy Walmsley, "World Prison Brief" (London: Institute for Criminal Policy Research, 2016).

3. "Statistics," United Nations Office on Drugs and Crime, available at www.unodc.org/unodc/en/data-and-analysis/statistics.html.

4. Dirk van Zyl Smit, Catherine Appleton, and Georgie Benford, "Introduction," in *Life Imprisonment and Human Rights*, eds. Dirk van Zyl Smit and Catherine Appleton (Portland, OR: Hart Publishing, 2016), 9.

5. Peter J. Tak, "Sentencing and Punishment in the Netherlands," in *Sentencing and Sanctions in Western Countries*, eds. Michael Tonry and Richard S. Frase (New York: Oxford University Press, 2001), 172.

6. Miranda Boone, "Imposed Versus Undergone Punishment in the Netherlands," *Electronic Journal of Comparative Law* 15, no. 1 (2011): 475–88.

7. Federal Law Gazette, "Act Concerning the Execution of Prison Sentences and Measures of Rehabilitation and Prevention Involving Deprivation of Liberty" (*Federal Law Gazette*, 2013).

8. Marc Howard, *Unusually Cruel: Prisons, Punishment, and the Real American Exceptionalism* (New York: Oxford University Press, 2017).

9. Maurice Chammah, "Can German Prisons Teach America How to Handle Its Most Violent Criminals?" *The Marshall Project*, June 18, 2015.

10. Chammah, "German Prisons."

11. Tapio Lappi-Seppälä, "Sentencing and Punishment in Finland: The Decline of the Repressive Ideal," in *Life Imprisonment and Human Rights*, eds. Dirk van Zyl Smit and Catherine Appleton (Portland, OR: Hart Publishing, 2016), 472.

12. Beatriz López Lorca, "Life Imprisonment in Latin America," in *Life Imprisonment and Human Rights*, eds. Dirk van Zyl Smit and Catherine Appleton (Portland, OR: Hart Publishing, 2016), 43–72.

13. Marie Gottschalk, "No Way Out? Life Sentences and the Politics of Penal Reform," in *Life Without Parole: America's New Death Penalty?* eds. Charles J. Ogletree Jr. and Austin Sarat (New York: New York University Press, 2012).

14. Andrea Huber, Olivia Rope, and Frances Sheahan, "Global Prison Trends 2017" (Penal Reform International, 2017).

15. Leigh Courtney, Sarah Eppler-Epstein, Elizabeth Pelletier, Ryan King, and Serena Lei, "A Matter of Time: The Causes and Consequences of Rising Time Served in America's Prisons" (Urban Institute, 2017).

16. Julian V. Roberts, Loretta J. Stalans, David Indermaur, and Mike Hough, *Populism and Public Opinion: Lessons from Five Countries* (Oxford: Oxford University Press, 2002).

17. Michael Tonry, *Sentencing Matters* (London: Oxford University Press, 1997).

18. Michael Tonry, "The Absence of Equality and Human Dignity Values Makes American Sentencing Systems Fundamentally Different from Those in Other Western Countries" (Legal Studies Research Paper Series Research Paper No. 16-08, University of Minnesota Law School, 2016), 18.

19. van Zyl Smit, Appleton, and Benford, "Introduction," 8–9.

20. Standard 18-6-1. General Principles, Sentencing (Criminal Justice Section). American Bar Association.

21. The American Law Institute, "Model Penal Code: Sentencing" (Proposed Final Draft, April 10, 2017), 143.

The Racial Meaning of Life

1. Ashley Nellis, "Still Life: America's Increasing Use of Life and Long-Term Sentences" (The Sentencing Project, 2017).

2. David C. Baldus, Charles Pulaski, and George Woodworth, "Comparative Review of Death Sentences: An Empirical Study of the Georgia Experience," *Journal of Criminal Law and Criminology* 74, no. 3 (1983): 661–753.

3. McCleskey v. Kemp, 481 U.S. 279 (1987).

4. North Carolina Racial Justice Act, 2009–2010 Session.

5. Michael L. Radelet and Glenn L. Pierce, "Race and Death Sentencing in North Carolina, 1980–2007," *North Carolina Law Review* 89, no. 6 (2011): 2119–60.

6. American Bar Association, "Three Death Sentences Overturned Under Racial Justice Act," *Death Penalty Representation Project Press* 6, no. 1 (2013): 1–2.

7. Kim Severson, "North Carolina Repeals Law Allowing Racial Bias Claim in Death Penalty Challenges," *New York Times*, June 5, 2013.

8. Ashley Nellis, "The Lives of Juvenile Lifers: Findings from a National Survey" (The Sentencing Project, 2012).

9. Leigh Courtney, Sarah Eppler-Epstein, Elizabeth Pelletier, Ryan King, and Serena Lei, "A Matter of Time: The Causes and Consequences of Rising Time Served in America's Prisons," (Washington, DC: Urban Institute, 2017).

10. Andrew Gelman, Alex Kiss, and Jeffrey Fagan, "An Analysis of the NYPD's Stop-and-Frisk Policy in the Context of Claims of Racial Bias," Columbia Public Law Research Paper no. 05-95 (2005).

11. Katherine Beckett, "Race, Drugs, and Policing: Understanding Disparities in Drug Delivery Arrests," *Criminology* 44, no. 1 (2006).

12. Todd D. Minton and Zhen Zeng, "Jail Inmates in 2015" (Washington, DC: Bureau of Justice Statistics, 2016).

13. Legislative Analyst's Office, "A Primer: Three Strikes—The Impact After More Than a Decade," Legislative Analyst's Office, last modified October 2005. www.lao.ca.gov/2005/3_strikes/3_strikes_102005.htm.

14. E. Ann Carson, "Prisoners in 2016" (Washington, DC: Bureau of Justice Statistics, 2018).

15. Data Analysis Unit, "Second and Third Striker Felons in the Adult Institution Population" (California: Department of Corrections and Rehabilitation, 2015).

16. Pew Research Center, "Shrinking Majority of Americans Support Death Penalty" (Pew Research Center, 2014).

17. Justin T. Pickett, Ted Chiricos, Kristin M. Golden and Marc Gertz, "Reconsidering the Relationship Between Perceived Neighborhood Racial Composition and Whites' Perceptions of Victimization Risk: Do Racial Stereotypes Matter?" *Criminology* 50, no. 3 (2012): 145–86, using data from: Federal Bureau of Investigation, "Crime in the United States, 2009," available at www2.fbi.gov/ucr/cius2009/data/table_43.html (Tbl. 43).

18. Ted Chiricos, Kelly Welch, and Marc Gertz, "Racial Typification of Crime and Support for Punitive Measures," *Criminology* 42, no. 2 (2004): 359–89.

19. Justin T. Pickett and Ted Chiricos, "Controlling Other People's Children: Racialized Views of Delinquency and Whites' Punitive Attitudes Toward Juvenile Offenders," *Criminology* 50, no. 3 (2012): 697, referencing

Barry C. Feld, *Bad Kids: Race and the Transformation of the Juvenile Court* (New York: Oxford University Press, 1999).

20. Michael Tonry, *Punishing Race: A Continuing American Dilemma* (New York: Oxford University Press, 2011).

The Meaning of Life for Criminal Justice Reform

1. Roy Walmsley. "World Prison Brief" (London: Institute for Criminal Policy Research, 2016).

2. Catherine Appleton, "Lone Wolf Terrorism in Norway," *International Journal of Human Rights* 18, no. 2 (2014): 127–42.

3. Sasha Abramsky, "The Dope Dealer Who Got 55 Years," *The Progressive*, May 31, 2006.

4. James P. Lynch and William Alex Pridemore, "Crime in International Perspective," in *Crime and Public Policy*, eds. James Q. Wilson and Joan Petersilia (Oxford: Oxford University Press, 2011), 5–52.

5. "Penalties for Drug Law Offences in Europe at a Glance," European Monitoring Centre for Drugs and Drug Addiction, available at www.emcdda .europa.eu/topics/law/penalties-at-a-glance.

6. National Research Council, *The Growth of Incarceration in the United States: Exploring Causes and Consequences* (Washington, DC: The National Academies Press, 2014), 53–55.

7. Alexia Cooper and Erica L. Smith, "Homicide Trends in the United States, 1980–2008" (Washington, DC: Bureau of Justice Statistics, 2011), 2.

8. National Research Council, *Growth of Incarceration*, 155.

9. Steven R. Belenko, *Harsh Justice: Crack and the Evolution of Anti-Drug Policy* (Westport, CT: Greenwood Press, 1993); United States Sentencing Commission, "Annual Report 1995" (United States Sentencing Commission 1995).

10. Jeremy Travis, "But They All Come Back: Rethinking Prisoner Reentry" (Washington, DC: U.S. Department of Justice, 2000).

11. Joan Petersilia, *When Prisoners Come Home: Parole and Prisoner Reentry* (Oxford: Oxford University Press, 2003); Travis, "But They All Come Back."

12. Marc Mauer, *Race to Incarcerate* (New York: The New Press, 2006).

13. The Sentencing Project, "U.S. Prison Population Trends 1999–2015: Modest Reductions with Significant Variation" (The Sentencing Project, May 2017).

14. Marie Gottschalk, *Caught: The Prison State and the Lockdown of American Politics* (New Jersey: Princeton University Press, 2014).

15. Gottschalk, *Caught*.

16. Ashley Nellis, "Still Life: America's Increasing Use of Life and Long-Term Sentences" (The Sentencing Project, 2017).

17. Leigh Courtney, Sarah Eppler-Epstein, Elizabeth Pelletier, Ryan King, and Serena Lei, "A Matter of Time: The Causes and Consequences of Rising Time Served in America's Prisons" (Urban Institute, 2017).

18. Ashley Nellis, "Life Goes On: The Historic Rise in Life Sentences in America" (The Sentencing Project, 2013), 1.

19. See *People v. Edward Hill* (2006), in which the Michigan Supreme Court ruled that the parole board's implementation of a "life means life" policy, beginning in 1992, did not violate the federal ex post facto clause by increasing the petitioner's sentence.

20. Jessica S. Henry, "Death-in-Prison Sentences: Overutilized and Underscrutinized," in *Life Without Parole: America's New Death Penalty?* eds. Charles J. Ogletree Jr. and Austin Sarat (New York: New York University Press, 2012), 69.

21. James Austin, John Clark, Patricia Hardyman, and Alan Henry, "Three Strikes and You're Out: The Implementation and Impact of Strike Laws" (National Institute of Justice, 2000).

22. American Civil Liberties Union, "A Living Death: Life Without Parole for Nonviolent Offenses" (American Civil Liberties Union, 2013), 2.

23. James Austin and Barry Krisberg, "Wider, Stronger and Different Nets: The Dialectics of Criminal Justice Reform," *Journal of Research in Crime and Delinquency* 18, no. 1 (1981): 165–96.

24. Three Strikes Project, "Proposition 36 Progress Report: Over 1,500 Prisoners Released, Historically Low Recidivism Rate" (Stanford Law School, 2014).

25. Jane Gross, "Born of Grief, 'Three Strikes' Laws Are Being Rethought," *New York Times*, July 3, 2011.

26. Three Strikes Project, "Proposition 36 Progress Report."

27. Ashley Nellis, "The Lives of Juvenile Lifers: Findings from a National Survey" (The Sentencing Project, 2012).

28. Nellis, "The Lives of Juvenile Lifers," 10–11.

29. Nellis, "The Lives of Juvenile Lifers," 9.

30. Graham v. Florida, 560 U.S. 48 (2010), quoting Roper v. Simmons, 543 U.S., at 570.

The Meaning of Life for Public Safety

1. American Friends Service Committee, *Struggle for Justice: A Report on Crime and Punishment in America* (New York: Hill & Wang, 1971), 151.

2. National Advisory Commission on Criminal Justice Standards and Goals, *Task Force Report on Corrections* (Washington, DC: National Criminal Justice Reference Service, 1973), 567.

3. National Advisory Commission, *Corrections*.

4. National Advisory Commission, *Corrections*, 567.

5. Rolf Loeber and David P. Farrington, "Age-Crime Curve," in *Encyclopedia of Criminology and Criminal Justice*, eds. Gerben Bruinsma and David Weisburd (New York: Springer, 2014), 12–18.

6. Howard N. Snyder, Alexia D. Cooper, and Joseph Mulako-Wangota, "Arrest Rates by Age for Robbery 2014" (Washington, DC: Bureau of Justice Statistics, 2017), generated using the Arrest Data Analysis Tool, October 26, 2017.

7. Marieke Liem, "Homicide Offender Recidivism: A Review of the Literature," *Aggression and Violent Behavior* 18 (2013): 19–25.

8. Robert Sampson and John Laub, "Life-Course Desisters? Trajectories of Crime Among Delinquent Boys Followed to Age 70," *Criminology* 41, no. 3 (2003): 301–40.

9. Roper v. Simmons, 543 U.S. 551 (2005).

10. "Commutations Granted by President Barack Obama (2009–2017)," The United States Department of Justice.

11. United States Sentencing Commission, *An Analysis of the Implementation of the 2014 Clemency Initiative* (Washington, DC: United States Sentencing Commission, 2017).

12. CNN, March 22, 2018, https://www.cnn.com/videos/politics/2018/03/22/jeff-sessions-attorney-general-drug-trafficking-death-penalty-sot.wctv.

13. Paul H. Robinson and John M. Darley, "Does Criminal Law Deter? A Behavioural Science Investigation," *Oxford Journal of Legal Studies* 24, no. 2 (2004): 173–205.

14. Jennifer Bronson, Jessica Stroop, Stephanie Zimmer, and Marcus Berzofsky, "Drug Use, Dependence, and Abuse Among State Prisoners and Jail Inmates, 2007–2009" (Washington, DC: Bureau of Justice Statistics, 2017).

15. Daniel Nagin, "Deterrence in the Twenty-First Century: A Review of the Evidence" (Working Paper, Carnegie Mellon University, 2013), 1–8.

16. Nagin, "Deterrence in the Twenty-First Century," 3.

17. Cesare Beccaria, *On Crimes and Punishments* (United States of America: Seven Treasures Publications, 2009).

18. Robert Weisberg, Debbie A. Mukamal, and Jordan D. Segall, *Life in Limbo: An Examination of Parole Release for Prisoners Serving Life Sentences*

with the Possibility of Parole in California (Stanford, CA: Stanford Criminal Justice Center, Stanford Law School, 2011).

19. Marc Mauer, Ryan King, and Malcolm Young, "The Meaning of 'Life': Long Prison Sentences in Context" (Washington, DC: The Sentencing Project, 2004).

20. Marieke Liem, "Homicide Offender Recidivism: A Review of the Literature," *Aggression and Violent Behavior* 18 (2013): 23.

21. E. Ann Carson and William J. Sabol, *Aging of the State Prison Population, 1993–2013* (Washington, DC: Bureau of Justice Statistics, 2016).

22. Peter W. Greenwood and Susan Turner, "Juvenile Crime and Juvenile Justice," in James Q. Wilson and Joan Petersilia, eds., *Crime and Public Policy* (New York: Oxford University Press, 2011), 88–129.

23. Raj Chetty, Nathaniel Hendren, and Lawrence Katz, "The Effects of Exposure to Better Neighborhoods on Children: New Evidence from the Moving to Opportunity Project," *American Economic Review* 106, no. 4 (2013): 855–902.

Enacting a Twenty-Year Maximum Sentence

1. The American Law Institute, "Model Penal Code: Sentencing" (Philadelphia: The American Law Institute, 2017), 164.

2. The American Law Institute, "Model Penal Code: Sentencing," 565.

3. R.E. "Bob" Brown, "A Beacon of Hope—Sunny Ways: Life Sentenced Offenders," *Executive Exchange* (Fall 2016).

4. Pamela M. Yates and Lynn Garrow, "Evaluation Report: Life Line Program" (Evaluation Branch of the Correctional Service of Canada, February 2010).

5. Laura Sullivan, "Life After 'Life': Aging Inmates Struggle for Redemption," National Public Radio (June 4, 2014).

6. "EJI's Post-Release Preparation and Education Program (PREP)" (Montgomery: Equal Justice Initiative), available online at https://eji.org/eji-prep-reentry-program, accessed September 26, 2017.

7. Andrew J. Harris, "Policy Implications of New York's Sex Offender Civil Management Assessment Process," *Criminology and Public Policy* 16, no. 3 (2017): 947.

8. Harris, "Policy Implications," 949.

9. Jeffrey C. Sandler and Naomi J. Freeman, "Evaluation of New York State's Sex Offender Civil Management Assessment Process Recidivism Outcomes," *Criminology and Public Policy* 16, no. 3 (2017): 915.

10. Montgomery v. Louisiana, 577 U.S.___ (2016).

11. Brown, et al. v. Plata, et al., 563 U.S. 493 (2011).

12. United States Sentencing Commission, "U.S. Sentencing Commission 2014 Drug Guidelines Amendment Retroactivity Data Report" (United States Sentencing Commission, October 2017).

13. J. Richard Couzens and Tricia A. Bigelow, "The Amendment of the Three Strikes Sentencing Law" (Barrister Press, May 2017), 124–25.

14. Susan B. Tucker and Eric Cadora, "Justice Reinvestment: To Invest in Public Safety by Reallocating Justice Dollars to Refinance Education, Housing, Healthcare, and Jobs," *Ideas for an Open Society* 3, no. 3 (November 2003).

15. The Pew Charitable Trusts, "31 States Reform Criminal Justice Policies Through Justice Reinvestment" (The Pew Charitable Trusts, January 2016).

16. Jazmine Ulloa, "Prop. 47 Got Thousands Out of Prison. Now, $103 Million in Savings Will Go Towards Keeping Them Out," *Los Angeles Times*, March 29, 2017.

17. Note that Japan does as well, but the annual number of executions is generally in the single digits. See Roger Hood and Carolyn C. Hoyle, *The Death Penalty: A Worldwide Perspective* (Oxford: Oxford University Press, 2015).

18. Death Penalty Information Center, "Facts About the Death Penalty" (Death Penalty Information Center, January 9, 2018).

19. Jordan Steiker and Carol Steiker, "The Death Penalty and Mass Incarceration: Convergences and Divergences," *American Journal of Criminal Law* 41, no. 2 (2014): 190.

20. Connecticut, Illinois, Maryland, Nebraska, New Jersey, New Mexico, and New York (Death Penalty Information Center, 2015).

21. New Jersey Death Penalty Study Commission, "New Jersey Death Penalty Study Commission Report" (New Jersey Death Penalty Study Commission, January 2007).

22. Ashley Nellis, "Life Goes On: The Historic Rise in Life Sentences in America" (The Sentencing Project, 2013), 16.

23. Jonathan R. Sorenson and Rocky L. Pilgrim, "An Actuarial Risk Assessment of Violence Posed by Capital Murder Defendants," *Journal of Criminal Law and Criminology* 90, no. 4 (2000): 1251–71.

24. Lake Research Partners, "Survey of Death Penalty Opinions, 2010." Survey results available online: http://www.deathpenaltyinfo.org/documents/topline.DPIC.DPNDP.pdf.

25. Brandon L. Garrett, "Claiming Innocence," *Minnesota Law Review* 92 (2008): 1629–1724.

26. Gill, "Clemency for Lifers," 21–26.

27. Tina Maschi, George Leibowitz, Joanne Rees, and Lauren Pappecena, "Analysis of US Compassionate and Geriatric Release Laws: Applying a

Human Rights Framework to Global Prison Health," *Journal of Human Rights Social Work* 1 (2016): 165–74.

The Future of Life in America

1. Michelle Alexander: *Mass Incarceration in the Age of Colorblindness* (New York: The New Press, 2012); Bryan Stevenson, *Just Mercy* (New York: Random House, 2014).

2. Ava DuVernay, *13th* (Netflix, 2016).

Marc Mauer is the executive director of The Sentencing Project, a national organization based in Washington, DC, that promotes criminal justice reform. The author of *Race to Incarcerate* and *Invisible Punishment* (both from The New Press), he lives in Silver Spring, Maryland.

Ashley Nellis is a senior research analyst for The Sentencing Project who has written extensively on the prevalence of life sentences in the United States. She lives in Falls Church, Virginia.

Kerry Myers served twenty-seven years of a life sentence for a crime he maintains he did not commit. He is the former editor of *The Angolite*, was the recipient of the Thurgood Marshall Journalism Award, and lives in Baton Rouge.

Publishing in the Public Interest

Thank you for reading this book published by The New Press. The New Press is a nonprofit, public interest publisher. New Press books and authors play a crucial role in sparking conversations about the key political and social issues of our day.

We hope you enjoyed this book and that you will stay in touch with The New Press. Here are a few ways to stay up to date with our books, events, and the issues we cover:

- Sign up at www.thenewpress.com/subscribe to receive updates on New Press authors and issues and to be notified about local events
- Like us on Facebook: www.facebook.com/newpress books
- Follow us on Twitter: www.twitter.com/thenewpress

Please consider buying New Press books for yourself; for friends and family; or to donate to schools, libraries, community centers, prison libraries, and other organizations involved with the issues our authors write about.

The New Press is a 501(c)(3) nonprofit organization. You can also support our work with a tax-deductible gift by visiting www.thenewpress.com/donate.